A REVOLUTION
COMPASSION

A REVOLUTION *of* COMPASSION

Faith-Based Groups as Full Partners in Fighting America's Social Problems

Dave Donaldson and Stanley Carlson-Thies

Baker Books

A Division of Baker Book House Co
Grand Rapids, Michigan 49516

© 2003 by Dave Donaldson and Stanley Carlson-Thies

Published by Baker Books
a division of Baker Book House Company
P.O. Box 6287, Grand Rapids, MI 49516-6287
www.bakerbooks.com

Printed in the United States of America

Library of Congress Cataloging-in-Publication Data
Donaldson, Dave.
    A revolution of compassion : faith-based groups as full partners in fighting America's social problems / by Dave Donaldson and Stanley Carlson-Thies.
        p.   cm.
    ISBN 0-8010-6445-7 (pbk.)
    1. Public welfare—United States—Religious aspects. 2. Human services—Contracting out—United States. 3. Church and social problems—United States. 4. Church charities—Government policy—United States. 5. Church charities—United States—Finance. I. Carlson-Thies, Stanley W. II. Title.
HV95.D66 2003
361.7′5′0973—dc21   2003009298

Scripture is taken from the HOLY BIBLE, NEW INTERNATIONAL VERSION®. NIV®. Copyright © 1973, 1978, 1984 by International Bible Society. Used by permission of Zondervan. All rights reserved.

Contents

Foreword

One of my most satisfying moments in Congress came the day the House passed the Community Solutions Act, also known as the faith-based bill. As a minister, I knew all too well that many in our society are afflicted by ills only the church can cure. My Democratic cosponsor, Representative Tony Hall, whose work with the poor and hungry had become noteworthy, was compelled by his dedication to those less fortunate to work on this legislation. But neither of us was prepared for the backlash we would encounter in trying to level the playing field for faith-based organizations to administer compassion—something they do naturally.

This bill had its roots in the 2000 presidential election cycle, when then presidential candidate George W. Bush talked about compassionate conservatism. Many clucked and tried to make a cynical attack on him. For me, however, it was native air. Long before the election I had talked about a new kind of conservatism—one that offered a hand up, not just a hand out. I talked about measuring compassion *not* by how many were on AFDC or welfare or in public housing but by how few were on these rolls because we had given them the means to get out of the rut of poverty.

In 1996, a Republican-led Congress passed the most sweeping welfare reform to date. It was so successful that years later social scientists were still scratching their heads about how we had done it. But we *had* done it. We were restoring dignity and pride in neighborhoods that others had written off. We were allowing people to open the gateway to the future for themselves and their families.

It was during the debate regarding the Community Solutions Act that I realized government could not do certain things as well as faith-based groups—things like drug rehab, curbing teen pregnancy, or even assisting with job training and job placement. You see, government treats the problem, while faith-based programs treat the whole individual. That, along with divine intervention, is the key to their overwhelming success. Many of us in government woke up to the reality that faith-based institutions all over this nation were feeding the hungry, giving clothes and shelter to the homeless, and putting people's lives back together just as the Good Shepherd had commanded. With that knowledge the president's faith-based and community initiative agenda fired up the spirit of the Community Solutions Act.

In those exhilarating days of working on the faith-based issue, I met the authors of this book. Never in the history of Congress had a coalition of this magnitude emerged among religious groups; people of all faiths joined together to rally the House of Representatives. This bill had the unprecedented support of more than sixteen hundred nonprofit organizations. Both authors, Dave Donaldson and Stanley Carlson-Thies, were instrumental in rallying the armies of compassion to spearhead this legislation through the U.S. House.

Our bill passed through the House but was declared dead on arrival in the Senate. Anti-faith groups had successfully won the minds and votes of enough Senators to make passage of the Community Solutions Act impossible. I'm glad that my colleagues Senators Rick Santorum (R-Pennsylvania) and Joseph Lieberman (D-Connecticut) believed enough in the importance of faith-based involvement to push fellow Senators to consider at least the CARE Act—a bill that represents progress even though it does not include all the Charitable Choice protections. The "anti" forces are against even this bill, sad to say. But I'm hopeful the day will come when the Senate and the House again will cooperate to pass legislation that makes federal programs more faith-friendly—as they should and must be.

This book is timely, well written, and well titled. There is a Revolution of Compassion in our nation to unite Americans who want to help the poor, addicted, hungry, and homeless—no matter what their race, religion, or background happens to be. I am well acquainted with the authors and their leadership role in this revolution. Stanley led President Bush's effort to establish faith-based offices in the federal agencies, and over the years Dave has become a confidant and close comrade in leading a diverse and influential group of faith-based leaders under the umbrella of We Care America. I know these men to be leaders in the area of combining compassion and expertise. I share their optimism that we can continue on this path to where government and corporations encourage the good deeds of the faith community and view faith-based groups as partners in the wars against poverty, teen pregnancy, and other social ills.

For this revolution to grow, it must be rooted in a commitment to the neighborhood and to faith-based organizations, to the people who have the same zip code as those who need the help. Americans agree overwhelmingly that public funds should go to the groups that are getting the best results. In many cases faith-based organizations are the most effective at addressing our nation's social brokenness.

Now that I am back in the private sector, my passion for this movement has not waned. I am convinced more than ever that the foundation of our country must be laid upon strong family values, unflappable character, and the determination to make life better for every citizen regardless of race or creed. I believe this book will serve a vital role in preserving and propelling this moral-biblical mandate to care for the neediest of our citizens. The authors have added great value to this movement by clearly and persuasively chronicling the past, present, and future challenges and opportunities for all Americans in this Revolution of Compassion.

J. C. Watts Jr.

Preface

Speak up for those who cannot speak for themselves, for the rights of all who are destitute. Speak up and judge fairly; defend the rights of the poor and needy.

Proverbs 31:8–9

My most vivid childhood memory is not a happy one. The events of an August night in 1969 transformed me from a carefree and mischievous California preacher's kid to a fatherless child, dependent for survival on kind-hearted friends and relatives—and from the U.S. government's welfare system.

That night my parents drove off for a church business meeting in Concord, California. Although it wasn't their habit to do so, they left us four children—Hal, Steve, Susan, and me—at home with a baby-sitter, an unusual decision that probably saved our lives. In any case, it wasn't long after they left when the familiar faces of church members began to show up at our front door, weeping and distressed.

The next thing we knew, the four of us were gently given the most heartbreaking news: a drunk driver had killed our beloved father in a traffic accident. Our mother had survived, but barely so. She was in grave condition—only alive because an emergency worker had made the agonizing choice to provide oxygen for her, not for her husband. "She looked more likely to survive," he had explained. The doctors later confirmed his decision—if he had provided oxygen to Dad instead, they both would have died.

Several weeks after Dad was killed, my mother returned home from the hospital. That night as I lay in my bed, I could hear her moaning in pain. I recall weeping into my pillow and asking, "God, how could you let this happen? How are we going to make it?" Dad was gone, the cupboards were empty, the closets practically bare, and my mother's body was held together with pins and plates.

I remember thinking, "Without our dad to make money, how are we going to buy food?" We didn't exactly have much to begin with. At the time of the accident my father had been pastoring a tiny church. Although it was growing steadily, the congregation was struggling even to pay him a living wage. The Christmas before, I had dreaded returning to school because the other kids always bragged about their gifts. I knew that when they asked me what I had received, I would have to conjure up some imaginary presents to avoid embarrassment.

Even before Dad died, I had been wearing shoes that were too small for my feet—my toes hurt, but I never told anyone because I knew there was no money for bigger shoes. For a while, we had lived in a motel because Dad had purchased a fixer-upper house that needed major work before we could occupy it. Dad had big dreams for our church and our new home, but once he died everything seemed lost.

That night as I lay in bed listening to my mother's battle with pain, I clung to some words I had heard in Sunday school, "God helps the widows and is a Father to the fatherless," but I wondered how he could possibly take care of us from heaven. I soon learned that God works through people—all kinds of people—to provide for those who need his help.

The days that followed my mother's return home are etched in my mind as if they happened yesterday. My grandmother, Reahn, moved in and inspired us with her smile, her faith, and her great French toast and chocolate cake. Our Uncle Jim took care of the business matters. Our church family also showered us with love and concern. I recall walking out to the mailbox and finding letters of encouragement and anonymous gifts of five dollars, twenty dollars, and one hundred dollars. Families brought us hot meals and groceries. In actual fact, the food was so good that when Mom began to recover we pleaded with people to keep bringing us meals.

Although my mother is a gifted person, she readily admits cooking is not her forte.

In addition to this wonderful help from family, friends, and neighbors, we received help from a place I never had thought much about. A government social worker visited our home and helped us complete paperwork so we could receive Medicaid and food stamps. This woman was warm and friendly, and she took a special interest in each of us. That government help was no substitute for the personal and loving compassion of church, family, and friends, but it gave us a crucial foundation of material goods and was really important in our family's recovery from this tragedy. I have never been a fan of big government, but I have always remembered what a blessing it was to our family that our nation's government exercises a responsibility toward families that have been plunged into economic need.

Three weeks after Mom's return, members of our church and neighborhood folks gathered at our dilapidated home for a work-day. Men painted the outside of the house, repaired windows, and planted bushes and trees. Women cleaned and oversaw the replacement of furniture, drapes, and appliances. By the end of that memorable Saturday, our house looked to us like it belonged in *Lifestyles of the Rich and Famous.*

I stood in the front yard and watched with amazement as these people served us without expecting anything in return. Something in my heart began to change. For the first time since the accident I no longer felt anger toward God or toward the drunk driver who had killed my father. Instead I thought, *We must be worth a lot for people to give up so much to help us.* In that moment—which I regard as an epiphany—I told myself, "I want to be like these people. I want to help others the way other people are helping us."

Within a year my mother was back on her feet and entering the job market. Although she was still debilitated and had not worked outside the home for over ten years, Dow Chemical accepted her in a job-training program. Despite physical pain and financial uncertainty, our mother never lost her faith in God or her passion to provide for her children. She proved herself to be far more than a survivor. Mom excelled, was promoted repeatedly, and became a lead buyer for Dow Chemical. She also founded a group to help widows through the grieving process.

In retrospect, I see our family as a testimony to the successful cooperation between public and private communities—the government with its social services, the corporate sector, neighbors, and the church family all reached out to us, and their combined efforts set our family back on its feet again. Without the compassionate service of these disparate but interdependent groups, my parents' tragic accident could have sent our wounded family into a vicious cycle of despair and poverty for generations to come.

Instead, the days that followed the accident and our slow but constant recovery shaped our future in positive and productive ways. Eventually all three Donaldson sons—Hal, Steve, and I— began a nonprofit organization called Convoy of Hope to provide food, clothing, medical screenings, and jobs for disadvantaged families whose circumstances had left them in need of help.

In 2001 I took another step and founded We Care America. Today we are working to empower churches and organizations with ministry models, resources, and volunteers. Because of what I experienced in my own family's recovery from crisis and what I have seen in other needy families' experiences, We Care America has a particular calling to challenge churches and parachurch social ministries to consider collaborating with other nonprofit organizations, with businesses, and with government programs. Constructed rightly, these collaborations can expand the reach of faith-based programs, providing help and hope to those who are struggling to survive. Because of what our family experienced, it has become my vision and mission to inspire other wounded healers to make an investment of time, talent, and resources. I believe that by using every possible means available, we can mobilize armies of compassion around the world.

The purpose of this book is to inspire and encourage you to join the revolution of compassion. We are called not only to love God with all our heart, soul, mind, and strength but also our neighbors as ourselves (Mark 12:30–31). Although this command to serve others has always been there, in our days it has a new urgency and opens up new opportunities. Government officials, business leaders, scholars, and the media think that people of faith and their service programs have something unique and essential to contribute to our society's effort to uplift the poor and to strengthen communities and families. Let's be sure our light is shining and not hidden and that our salt is salty and not useless.

As you ponder and pray about how you and your church can be better servants to the hurting in your community, you may be wondering what to do about the invitation of political leaders for church-based programs to partner with government, the growing interest of corporations and foundations to support faith-based charities, and the outreach of traditional service organizations like the Red Cross, Goodwill, and the United Way to churches and parachurch ministries. We've written this book to be a guide for you, whether you are an interested layperson, a minister, the leader of or a participant in a faith-based nonprofit organization, or a Christian legislator or civil servant.

What is this faith-based initiative? Can Christians trust it? Will it just disappear tomorrow? What about government money? Isn't it dangerous? And what good can come out of collaborating with secular groups or with Christians of other denominations? We, the authors, are in the church, our experience is in Christian parachurch ministries, and we have helped to shape the policies and plans of the faith-based initiative. We are convinced that this is the time for Christians to step forward, boldly yet with discernment. New opportunities are available for us to serve our neighbors in the name of our Lord. In this book, we will help guide you to understand these new opportunities and to overcome the pitfalls. We invite you to join with us in the revolution of compassion.

Dave Donaldson

Acknowledgments

We first would like to thank our wives and families for their support and for cheerfully yielding all the extra hours that planning, writing, rewriting, and rewriting again consumed. Thanks to Kristy, Breahn, David, and Brooke Donaldson, and Christiane and Simon Carlson-Thies. Dave Donaldson also would like to thank especially his mother, Betty Foote, and grandmother, Reahn Hubin, who showed how God can take the wounded and turn them into wounded healers.

A huge thanks to Lela Gilbert who helped us, as she has helped many other Christian authors, by turning our inarticulate passages into readable ones, challenging us to speak from our hearts, melding two voices into one, and herding us so that we would stick to the tight writing schedule. Thank you to Robert Hosack and Chad Allen, our editors at Baker, who caught the importance and urgency of the book and worked so efficiently and enthusiastically to get it ready for release. Our grateful thank-you also goes to Calvin Edwards, who hatched the idea for this book with Dave Donaldson in discussions soon after George W. Bush became president and declared his intention to "rally the armies of compassion." We also heartily thank the leaders who generously answered our questions in interviews conducted by phone, in person, or by e-mail. Thank you to Shanti Feldhahn for conducting many of these and to Kristy Donaldson for transcribing the voice interviews.

Most of all, we want to thank the "doers," whose ideas, inspiration, and labors make up the "revolution of compassion." Some of them have names that appear in the news and others are known only to their friends, to those they help, and to God. Some operate small programs in out-of-the-way places; others manage large organizations with multiple local affiliates. Some are church leaders; others direct or work for nonprofits; some are in business; others are in foundations. Some of them are political leaders or civil servants. To all of them, who have chosen to use their talents and creativity and energy in the service of their neighbors as an expression of their love of God, we give our thanks.

1

America Needs a Revolution

> *Government clearly has had a role in undermining*
> *civil society. Families, churches, and community groups*
> *were forced to surrender their authority and function to*
> *bureaucratic experts. Fathers were replaced by welfare*
> *checks, private charities were displaced by government*
> *spending, religious volunteers were dismissed as "ama-*
> *teurs," whole communities were demolished in slum-*
> *clearance projects. The power to replace an institution is*
> *the power to destroy it.*
>
> Former Senator Dan Coats (R-Indiana)

America needs a Revolution of Compassion—a more effective way to help people and communities in need. In many ways, this revolution is already taking place, but as a society, we have a long way to go. Civil Rights leader and pastor Dr. Martin Luther King Jr. once wrote, "A social movement that only moves people is merely a revolt. A movement that changes both people and institutions is a revolution."[1] So what mind-sets need to be changed? What institutions need to be transformed for America to demonstrate genuine and active compassion?

The federal Health and Human Services budget is hundreds of billions of dollars annually—equivalent to that of the fourth largest country in the world. Other federal departments and state, county, and city governments run hundreds of other welfare and social programs. Yet, despite billions of dollars of spending to combat poverty and social problems and despite an economy that until recently had generated jobs and wealth consistently for many years, many of our fellow citizens live lives of poverty and despair. Recently the Census Bureau reported that poverty was once again increasing in the United States, up to 11.7 percent of the population—32.9 million poor Americans—in 2001. What has gone wrong in this wealthy, well-educated nation?

Topping the list of answers is the decline in personal responsibility of many Americans and the reluctance of too many churches to serve their needy neighbors as they should. In his presidential campaign book, *A Charge to Keep,* George W. Bush wrote, "The new culture said if people were poor, the government should feed them. If someone had no house, the government should provide one. Every social problem suddenly demanded a government solution."[2]

Government does have a proper place; it is a gift of God to curb oppression and promote justice. Yet government is no substitute for caring neighbors and friends, thriving businesses that provide jobs and careers, nonprofit programs that respond to emergencies and offer essential services, and faith-based organizations that show God's love as they teach skills or help a person escape an addiction.

Since his inauguration, President George W. Bush has promoted faith-based and grassroots programs as vital elements of our nation's response to need, and he has set out a vision of a new federal social policy that will extensively collaborate with such "neighborhood healers." However, the movement to build partnerships between government and faith-based organizations—and also businesses and secular charities—was under way before President Bush took office.

Around the nation and around the world, officials realize they have no monopoly on compassion. Indeed, a compassionate response to need must incorporate community groups, including

Government Agencies as Hope Centers?

The Hubert Humphrey Health and Human Services building stands in the shadow of the U.S. Capitol in Washington, D.C.—a block-long slab of cement with hundreds of tiny windows. Standing outside, I (Dave) watched as countless federal employees appeared and disappeared from my view. Some were on the phone; others sat at their computers. Suddenly, I was struck with the reality that for millions of Americans, this is where they go for help. This is their church, their synagogue, their cathedral, or their temple. Government workers have replaced their priests and rabbis, their pastors and spiritual counselors, to fulfill life-sustaining roles as caregivers and mentors.

As I walked inside, bustling groups of employees and visitors were passing through security and entering the catacombs of offices. On one side of the building I saw the pictures of President George W. Bush, Vice President Dick Cheney, and Health and Human Services Secretary Tommy Thompson. On the other side, Senator Hubert Humphrey's inspiring words blanket the wall, "The moral test of government is how it treats those who are in the dawn of life, the children; those who are in the twilight of life, the aged; and those who are in the shadows of life—the sick, the needy and the handicapped."

Just by stepping through the door, I too had entered the catacombs. My purpose was to meet with a compassionate federal employee. The question on the table: How can churches and parachurch organizations better partner with Health and Human Services to serve those in need?

Although officials have been talking a lot about wanting to work much more extensively with faith-based organizations, I'll admit that I was a bit skeptical about talking with a bureaucrat that day. I had also been a bit skeptical about whether many of America's faith-based groups were ready to step up to the challenge of service and partnership. Yet I knew the attempt to build a bridge between government and churches was an opportunity that must not be missed. The government employee stressed that "the mission of the faith- and community-based initiative was to remove the barriers between the needy and effective faith-based programs."

I walked out of her office asking myself, How can I persuade religious groups that are suspicious of government to consider this invitation seriously? More important: How can churches, synagogues, and other religious organizations be restored to their proper role, offering hope as well as help to the needy?

churches and other houses of worship, as well as nonprofit organizations that are defined and shaped by faith. Welfare, social services, job training, and justice programs are all being redesigned to be collaborative, to include businesses, charities, grassroots groups, and faith-based programs. Officials use different terms, but they all see that what people in distress often need is not only help but also hope. If that is the reality, then faith communities have to be part of the answer.

A NEW OPPORTUNITY

Are faith communities ready to be part of the answer? Are churches that profess Jesus Christ as Lord and the Bible as their guide for action as well as belief ready to play a central role in our nation's response to need?

Rather than demonstrate a readiness to respond, we all too often would rather simply blame the government for our nation's social ills. How many times have we heard: "If government hadn't taken the social services away from the church, we wouldn't be in this mess." As you will see in the next chapter, the story isn't like that at all. Early in our nation's history the government cooperated with churches and faith-based social services and took the leading place only when religious groups proved unwilling and unable to carry such a large responsibility. Government welfare did become too big, ineffective, and secular, but officials have been working to reform those mistakes since the mid-1990s.

A better question is this: Why have so many churches—unfettered in this country to be as generous as they wish toward their hurting neighbors—done so little to help the poor? This is particularly puzzling if their leaders were so convinced that government welfare was ineffective and harmful. We mean no blanket complaint. There are many churches (as well as synagogues, mosques, and temples) both large and small, in the suburbs, in inner cities, and out in the country that serve the needy generously, creatively, and effectively. In fact numerous studies have shown that almost all houses of worship provide at least a few different kinds of services to their neighbors who need help. Beyond congregations themselves, religious people have organized a wide variety of parachurch ministries—faith-based nonprofits—to provide specialized help across the range of needs, from homelessness to addiction, language difficulties, and health concerns.

If we are honest, though, we surely have to hear as a rebuke our Lord's reminder that the second commandment, subordinate only to the requirement to love God totally, is "Love your neighbor as yourself" (Mark 12:29–31). Surely we cannot blame the government for our self-preoccupation, our love of the world's treasures, or the evangelical church's slow recovery from its near abandonment nearly a century ago of social concern in its fight against the social gospel and theological liberalism.

Interview on 14 November 2002 with Rev. Dan de Leon, senior pastor, Templo Calvario, Santa Ana, California, the largest bilingual church in the United States

Q: President George W. Bush and other government officials often speak enthusiastically about wanting new partnerships with churches and other faith-based organizations, but some religious leaders have been very critical. In your view, why have some pastors been so unenthusiastic about the faith-based initiative?

A: I think suspicion has come especially from the evangelical Christian community. For a long time, what we heard from pulpits and learned in Bible schools and seminaries is that you can never mix the church with the government. Years ago, you would never find Hispanic evangelicals involved in politics. It was an absolute no-no. Our leaders felt that you would be compromising your convictions. Somehow your Christianity was going to be left out. It would be secularism all the way. With that mentality, we stayed away from government and politics.

However, some of us have had a different experience. We've been educated about politics, have been to the White House once or twice, have established relationships with government officials at the city, county, state, or national level. We've seen that it is possible to be a Christian and be involved in politics and be involved with the government. What we say now is, do not hesitate to participate—but be sure not to compromise your Christian, biblical convictions.

Today the whole environment of church and state has changed. There is a new way of seeing things, a new view of the church's role in society. I believe the Lord put us here to be more than a church on the corner that opens its doors for worship on Sunday morning and then closes the doors and has nothing else to do during the week. God has called us to build his kingdom and to win hearts for him but also to be light and salt in our world.

Light gives direction—it reveals and gives insight and understanding. I believe we have insightful information to give from God to our community concerning truth, peace, love, and reconciliation. We are also to be salt. Salt holds back deterioration. So where do we need to be? Where problems fester; where there is darkness. So we've come to realize we have a real function in this world, otherwise God would've taken us home.

I often say this: if I'm part of the problem, then I should also be part of the solution. If I'm part of American society with its problems, then I should be part of the solution. I cannot say: Oh, I've got my ticket in my pocket and I'm on my way to heaven, so forget about those problems all around me. I'm here to do something to help benefit the society of which I'm a part.

Q: If a church decides to be "part of the solution" and to reach out in community service in partnership with government, how should it prepare for the complexities of government funding?

A: Number one, we have to get our books in order. Every church in America that plans to get involved with government funding had better make sure it has its books in order. Churches have to make sure that they're operating properly and have a good record of keeping books, distributing funds properly, and so on.

If a Christian group is going to consider getting money from the government, they need to have a 501(c)(3) nonprofit organization separate from the church. It's just a clean way of making sure the funds do not mix in any way and create problems for the church or for the government down the road. We as local pastors and leaders are going to have to be very bright and intelligent on how we're going to get properly organized so that government funds do not become a stumbling block. Most of our churches don't know how to do this right. They need help.

Second, we need to pull together. Strength is in numbers. We have to come together and form a coalition or partnerships to be able to achieve things beyond our own little programs. We need a community effort, many people, a broad spectrum of the faith-based community, including some dialogue and even partnerships with religions that we have not worked with very well in the past. We have to be open to them because the government is not going to say, "We're only going to work with the evangelical community." Instead they are always talking of the faith-based community in general. We are going to have to be very smart, very intelligent on how we partner across faiths. Obviously, to some pastors, this is a no-no. They could never see themselves in the same room with people of other faiths. But if we're going to get government funds, we're going to have to find common ground with others for the common good of our communitites.

The third thing: we need to work with organizations such as We Care America. The government does not have enough money, people, or training programs to be able to work with every church in America. It doesn't even have time to meet with fifteen, twenty, thirty, or forty churches. We're going to have to find organizations that are well organized and able to handle large sums of money that can serve as intermediaries between the government and the local churches. I think this is one of our greatest needs, and WCA is one of our blessings because it provides a structure through which government funds can be accessed to be used in our communities.

Nor can we blame the government for how ineffective too much of the church's social outreach has been. Amy Sherman has traveled the United States widely to see how churches serve the poor, and she has also helped lead her own congregation's inner-city ministry. She points out that church social services often have been no better than government welfare, giving people material goods when they need a change in life. In a major article in *Christianity Today,* she called for "Church Welfare Reform," provocatively but persuasively arguing, "The church needs welfare reform every bit as much as the government did."[3] We add our voices to her call to churches and parachurch ministries to rededicate themselves to becoming as wise about assistance programs as they are dedicated to sharing the gospel.

A CHALLENGE TO PARTNERSHIP

We specifically challenge Christians to think of government in welfare and social services as an ally and partner, not as a competitor or enemy. Churches and faith-based social services, we are convinced, have an indispensable role to play if social assistance is to be as effective as the needy deserve. That role is usually best conceived as partnership with other organizations that are fulfilling their own responsibilities to be a good neighbor. Think of it this way: a person or family in deep need—a family like Dave's after his father's death—usually requires multiple kinds of help. While a church or a parachurch ministry may be able to provide some of the help needed, it is unlikely that any single organization can provide all the help that ought to be available.

A church-based program may give excellent job training and also the life-skills courses that can help a person become able to juggle home responsibilities with work tasks. None of this makes much difference, however, unless some business has a job to offer and someone, or some group, can help the person make the connection to that business. Or a church may give great help to a family in designing and keeping to a budget but be unable to assist them to locate, qualify for, and pay for decent and affordable housing. Or the parachurch ministry has a superior record helping moms on welfare prepare not only for their first job but for a sustainable career, but it has neither the ability nor the legal authority to require the absent fathers to pay the child support they owe their children.

Christian groups that want to be effective need to look first to see who else is busy serving and then prayerfully discern whether their best role might be to support those other organizations. Or if a new program is needed, they need to look around to find out which groups are providing the many other services that will also be needed—from money, to specialized programs, to advocacy to motivate a city agency to do the right thing.

Churches and parachurch ministries are part of the social safety net and must be considered full participants. Yet the social safety net has many other components, from large national nonprofits like the Red Cross and Goodwill, to local branches of national religiously affiliated organizations like the Salvation Army, Lutheran Services, Catholic Charities, and Jewish Federations, to local social agencies and clubs, to federal, state, and local government agencies. Businesses also play an integral role, not only by helping to support these other agencies but by providing jobs and pay.

In this book we will show that churches can best serve their hurting neighbors in collaboration with other groups—not only with other churches, but with secular and religiously affiliated nonprofit agencies, with businesses, and also with government. That's right—even in collaboration with government. Collaborating with government, by being connected in a referral relationship, and even by accepting government funds and being an approved service provider, helps groups sharpen up their services and their own organization.

Taking part in a referral network enables the faith-based group to easily point the person or family to additional services that only government might provide. Government funds might be the way the faith-based organization becomes able to increase the number of people it serves or to expand or improve the services it offers. Becoming part of the government-funded service network may be the only way the faith-based group can provide its services to people who are receiving government-mandated help.

Government officials are reaching out to America's faith communities, seeking new partners that can offer personal, transformative, and long-lasting assistance. After decades of ignoring groups that serve their neighbors in the name of the Lord, or inviting them to collaborate only if they were willing to mask their faith basis, government officials across the land are looking to faith-based groups with hope, and for hope.

What will Christians who love the Lord and their neighbors say in response?

SELLING OUR SOULS FOR GOVERNMENT MONEY?

Christians often counter with a question of their own: Won't collaboration with government require us to agree to suppress or abandon our faith? We've all heard the stories. *World* magazine once reported that a New York homeless shelter, after having been given several surplus refrigerators by a state official, was informed that it was now barred from sharing the gospel![4]

John Carr, Secretary of the Department of Social Development and World Peace (rather a daunting responsibility, as he jokes) for the U.S. Council of Catholic Bishops, reports that officials in Prince George's County, Maryland, were willing to fund the Archbishop Carroll shelter for the homeless only after the first part of the name was dropped. "And so now it's called Carroll House by everyone else and Archbishop Carroll House by us."[5]

The United Methodist Children's Home in Decatur, Georgia, was sued in mid–2002 not for mistreating the children in its charge or for wasting government money. No, it was sued because it insisted on its faith standards and refused to hire a Jewish counselor and because it fired a youth worker who violated its faith-based employment standards by declaring herself to be a lesbian.

Without a doubt, it's a dangerous world out there. Christian ministries must be not only "gentle as doves" but "wise as serpents" when they consider applying for government funding and status as a government-approved provider of services. Yet dangers are only part of the story. In fact, the story is becoming more and more positive as government attitudes are changing from hostility to hospitality toward faith-based organizations. For the important trend in welfare and social services is not merely that government officials are now welcoming faith-based providers but that they are actively modifying the rules and practices that made partnership a risky relationship for organizations jealous of their spiritual mission and religious character.

In the chapters that follow we will trace the history of government's changing attitude toward collaborating with faith-based social services. We will show the many ways the federal, state, and local governments are revising their programs and regulations to create equal opportunity for faith-based programs to compete for their funding—without having to abandon their faith basis. We will describe the social sector—the secular and religiously affiliated nonprofit organizations like Goodwill and the Salvation Army that, along with government, have traditionally comprised the major parts of the social safety net and that now often are searching for more fruitful relationships with churches and other houses of worship as well as with faith-based nonprofit programs. We will point out the critical role played by businesses, not only in helping to fund many services to the needy but in giving former welfare recipients and former prisoners jobs that enable them to attain self-sufficiency. We will also show how government officials are changing the way they run their programs and decide on grants and contracts so that there is a level playing field for faith-based as well as with secular organizations.

American society and government has not always been uniformly and resolutely anti-faith, and American society and government have not now become uniformly and resolutely pro-faith. Some bad practices and attitudes have changed; others have not. Some federal programs have become very open to collaborating with religious service providers, and others have not. The picture at the state, county, and city levels is similarly mixed.

Even when a United Way, state welfare agency, or major corporation has changed from suspicion of faith-based services to support, that change does not mean that church leaders or program directors can stop praying, ignore wise legal advice, or cease cultivating spiritual maturity among staff, volunteers, and board. Government and other partners can surely tempt a faith-based organization to become faithless by imposing antireligious requirements. But no matter how faith-friendly those outside powers want to be, they cannot force the faith-based organization to remain faithful. That is something only the organization itself—and its supporters and God—can make happen.

So these chapters will not only show how the environment for service by churches and parachurch ministries is being positively transformed. They will also propose ways that faith-based organizations can guard and enhance their faithfulness to God.

American society and government have placed before America's faith communities a great opportunity: the chance to play a much larger role in the social safety net and in the lives of the hurting as partners with other service organizations. The opportunity brings with it many challenges. Faith-based ministries cannot evade the question: Are they ready to seize the opportunity by expanding their service to neighbors in collaboration with government and other social institutions? Also, are they prepared to surmount the temptations to faithlessness that accompany collaboration?

Interview on 25 November 2002 with Bishop George McKinney, Church of God in Christ Worldwide, St. Stephen's Church, San Diego, California

---

Q: Bishop McKinney, why is it important that the government reach out to faith-based groups and find better ways to work with them?

A: I believe that faith-based agencies in cooperation with the government and the private sector can address the problems of homelessness, unemployment and under-employment, and crime and rehabilitation. The whole gamut of social and economic problems can be better addressed when the various resources of this great nation sit at the table together and work out the means of addressing problems in order to improve the quality of life for all of our citizens. It has to be done. It's urgent. Otherwise we will continue to have a growing population of the disaffected and the homeless, and our prisons will continue to be one of the government's major housing programs. The problem is that the government's social services do not have a built-in structure for rehabilitation, for forgiveness, for redirection, for redemption. That element is just not present in the government, but the faith-based community has a great and strong belief in redemption, reconciliation, and new beginnings. That has been the missing element in government programs. It's important, it's critical for all of the society's resources to come together and work for the good of the nation, for the good of every citizen.

Q: How do you assess the suspicion of some black leaders about the President's faith-based initiative and about churches partnering with the government?

A: There are still major denominational leaders who are very suspicious of entering into any kind of contract with the government because of their fear of tax auditors and their fear of being silenced on political issues. There's a very strong feeling that if an agency or denomination starts receiving funds from the government, there will be the loss of freedom to speak truth to power. That's a very real concern. Because of that concern, some major denominational leaders are encouraging their public, their participants, their organizations to stay away from the faith-based initiative altogether.

On the other hand, it is my sense, it is my feeling that while these are real concerns, I think the faith-based leader is called to have strength and courage and the integrity to respond to human suffering and to use whatever resources are available and not to lose courage to speak the truth. That's sometimes a tightrope, but I think we are called to walk that tightrope.

There can be a real temptation for those who have struggled for years to do social, educational, or rehabilitative work with hardly any support, and suddenly funds are available. It can be very exciting. Being human, we have the tendency to seek that easy path and to leave behind some of the anxiety and pain we've all experienced in delivering services with inadequate resources. So the danger is that we can become seduced by the funding source. That's a danger we must live with. Now if one cannot handle that seduction, then it is better to stay away. But if one has the maturity and understands that one can maintain integrity and can deliver services with the resources that are available from the corporate community and the government, I feel that we ought to go for it.

This book will help you understand both the opportunities and the challenges. It will also help you see how to confront temptations. We do not pretend to offer a complete survey here. This short book is a starting point on a journey to greater service. We invite you to prayerfully discern the signs of the times and to see whether your church and the parachurch ministries you support or lead should join the Revolution of Compassion by expanding their efforts—in collaboration with others.

A SCANDAL IN THE CHURCH'S BACKYARD

Years ago, I (Dave) participated in a distribution of food by a church. As I helped, I tried to get acquainted with the families who came looking for help. I wanted to be friendly. Besides that, I wanted to refer people with special needs to church programs and to government assistance for ongoing care. I asked, for example, if the families had a place to live, what school the children attended, or if any members had medical needs.

As I handed groceries to one woman and her child, I asked, "Do you and your little girl have a place to live?"

To my astonishment, she pointed to a hidden area located behind the church's dumpster. "We live there," she said quietly.

It was hard for me to believe, so I repeated, "You live there behind the church?"

"Yes," she replied with a sheepish look. "I accepted Jesus at this church and asked for help, but I never heard anything from anyone after that." With her eyes filling with tears she continued, "I was too dirty to go into the church, so I decided to live close by because it's safer for my child."

What a scandal. This woman was living in the backyard of the church and neither the pastors nor the parishioners knew it! To make matters worse, when I brought this woman's story to the attention of the church leaders, they tried to blame the woman for not fitting in.

If the church is to be part of the contemporary Revolution of Compassion, it cannot condemn the needy or blame the government. God calls us to compassion for others who need our help. As Amy Sherman has written,

> God's concern for the poor is no footnote in scripture; no mere afterthought. It is a central, pervasive theme. Over 400 verses— sprinkled throughout every genre of scripture, from the Law to the wisdom literature and from the prophets to the Gospels and the epistles—speak about God's passion for the needy and His desire that His followers share that passion. One researcher decided to physically cut out, with scissors, every reference in scripture to God's heart for the poor. He ended up with a very "hole-y" Bible indeed; it was literally shot through with holes. Whenever we are passionate about something, we talk about it often. God, through His Word, speaks frequently about the poor and needy. Undoubtedly, He has "regard for the poor" [Psalm 41:1]—and wants us to as well.[6]

It is inarguable that the church must be compassionate. The argument of the following chapters is that the church, to be as effective as possible in its compassion, should seize today's opportunity to collaborate with businesses, charities, and government. America needs a revolution!

2

The Roots of Revolution

I think churches are in touch . . . on a different level than
those who are just in a training program. The spiritual
connection may help the clients get past some of the other
barriers. They know there are some other areas they
could get assistance from the church. I truly think that
because churches are a foundation of a community, they
have many tools available to help folks. And that's really
what our department wants to do anyway.

Bryon Noon, Bureau of Employment
and Training, Pennsylvania Department
of Welfare—the program monitor overseeing
Neighborhood Joy Ministries, Cookman
United Methodist Church, Philadelphia

A surprising thing happened in Washington, D.C., in the summer of 1996. For decades the federal government had control of how the nation assists poor children, women, and families. Now Congress and President Bill

Clinton changed the course of welfare. In the welfare reform bill the president signed into law that August, state and local governments took over from Congress the chief responsibility for deciding how government can best help dependent families. The main effort of welfare was changed from financial aid to poor families into assistance designed to enable families to become self-supporting. Also, instead of presuming that government is the best provider of help, the new law encouraged welfare officials to team up with businesses, with private charities—and with churches and faith-based service organizations.

What a change! Although congregations and parachurch ministries have been serving their neighbors since long before federal welfare, their efforts for many decades were marginalized, said to be too unprofessional, too small-scale—and too religious. Although the government funded some programs connected to religious groups, that was simply because officials thought they could ignore the religion. The new welfare law, however, had a "Charitable Choice" section, requiring officials to evaluate faith-based providers of welfare help "on the same basis" as secular groups.

Since 1996 Congress has written the same invitation into several other federal programs as well. Not just the federal government, but also states, counties, and cities are looking to America's faith communities for new allies in the fight against poverty, drug addiction, juvenile delinquency, and other problems. Officials are also looking to secular grassroots groups, like neighborhood clubs and after-school programs, and to companies that are willing to reach out to former welfare recipients or prisoners who have turned their lives around. Corporations and foundations, which often have looked down on small community groups—especially religious ones—are realizing that they have to get over their prejudices if they want to support the most effective helpers in distressed neighborhoods.

How did this sharp change in course come about, and why did it take so long? Why were we on the other path in the first place? Why was government so dominant, and how is it being forced back? Why were faith-based services pushed to the margins, and why are they now being invited back into the center?

THE EARLY DAYS OF AMERICAN CHARITY

Most Americans think of welfare and programs to deal with juvenile crime, addictions, or the homeless as chiefly the government's responsibility. Earlier in our history, however, we had a different idea. Before government got involved in a large-scale and systematic way, beginning with the New Deal of the 1930s, a large part of the help for people in distress came from private groups, many of them religious.[1]

America has a rich history of neighbors helping neighbors, often in the name of Christ. That history was neglected until studies such as Marvin Olasky's *The Tragedy of American Compassion* expanded the focus beyond the growth of government welfare.[2] Still, the true story shouldn't be such a surprise. Americans have always been a religious people, and the faiths that have shaped the nation—especially Christianity and Judaism—teach that love of God requires love of neighbor.

Alexis de Tocqueville, that perceptive Frenchman who toured America in 1831, pointed out that Americans are inclined to solve problems by forming associations. In other countries, he noted, when something needed to be done, either government or some "great lord" would take the lead. In contrast, Americans "constantly unite," coming together in associations to promote a cause or respond to a need.[3]

Among the countless examples of how faith and the impulse to join with others spurred Americans to respond in an organized way to the needs of their neighbors was the Chicago Orphan Asylum, which was organized by Protestant congregations when a cholera epidemic in the mid-nineteenth century orphaned many children in Chicago. Jewish women from synagogues in New York City formed child-care programs, sewing schools, and employment services. Catholics, who immigrated to the United States in large numbers in the last quarter of the century, developed an extensive network of services. African-Americans, liberated from slavery but not accepted fully into society, started their own churches, which were community centers for social services and cultural activities as well as worship. Evangelicals, in the forefront of reform activities in the nineteenth century, started rescue missions in many big-city slums to provide meals and beds as well as the gospel.

This flourishing private and religious response to need did not mean that government was absent. In fact, the early colonists had brought from England the Poor Law system that required local officials to ensure a floor of support—although often a very inadequate floor—for destitute families and individuals. America's social safety net, in other words, included from the beginning not only churches and charities but also government. In earlier days in the South, there were no sharp lines between these institutions, and Anglican clergy were the administrators of the relief system run by local governments.

There is a good reason why local governments were involved with social support in this nation of believers, volunteers, and charities. Back in the early 1700s, Jonathan Edwards was the premier Protestant apologist and theologian at the time of the first Great Awakening, before the American Revolution, when thousands came to Christ, often at open-air meetings under the preaching of George Whitefield. Edwards wrote a sermon on *Christian Charity* that reminded believers that a true love of God would overflow into love of neighbor, as the Scriptures require.

Generous hearts were not enough, however, Edwards urged; government also had a role. That is because, "in this corrupt world," the hearts of Christians as well as unbelievers are distorted by sin, and so voluntary assistance can only be "an uncertain thing." Yet people who are destitute must be able to count on others helping them. Because voluntary charity is "precarious" and not an assured source of help, Edwards said, the colonial legislature was right to obligate town officials to provide assistance to the poor.[4]

In the decades after Edwards wrote, government's social role grew slowly. After the Civil War, the federal government granted pensions to veterans and their dependents. Early in the twentieth century, some states started offering support to widows and organizing workmen's compensation programs for people no longer able to work due to illness or injury.

Government expansion had several causes. For one thing, Americans' views about what government can and should do, and what churches and private charities ought to accomplish, were changing. Needs also were changing, and private efforts could not always keep up. With people moving from farms to the cities and the economy becoming more complex, families became more dependent on a cash income for current needs and for retirement, and more vulnerable to economic downturns. At the same time, the opportunity and impulse to help families who fell into crisis was diminishing. As cities expanded and companies became larger and more complex, people had less time to volunteer. The haves and have-nots became increasingly separated from each other.

The proliferation of denominations and faiths did not help, either. In 1877 Pastor Samuel Gurteen started the Buffalo Charity Organization Society to make private charity more effective by joining churches into a citywide system, following the successful plan of Rev. Thomas Chalmers in Glasgow, Scotland, but the plan didn't work here. Churches assigned to particular neighborhoods were inclined to first help their own members, but their assigned areas actually contained needy folks belonging to many different churches, or to none.[5] Denomination had to be downplayed if charity was to be effective, as Christian compassion requires.

Still, into the early years of the twentieth century, the American social safety net was both private and public. It incorporated both charities and government services and included many faith-based organizations. Religious and secular groups provided essential help to hurting neighbors, extending far beyond government programs. Charities often pioneered ideas and services, which government sometimes adopted. Our system of responding to needs was anchored in local governments and included many private groups, including religious organizations.

THE NEW DEAL

When the Great Depression followed the October 1929 stock market crash, America's social safety net quickly developed gaping holes. Thousands of banks failed; tens of thousands of companies collapsed. Within three years, one out of four workers was unemployed. Millions of Americans no longer had a regular income and turned to selling pencils or apples on street corners, riding the rails in the hope of finding food or work someplace across the country, or joining long breadlines. As needs mushroomed, money to supply help shriveled. Between 1929 and 1932, a third of America's private charities simply collapsed for lack of income. State and local governments were overwhelmed, too.

The New Deal was President Franklin Delano Roosevelt's response to the emergency. Federal initiatives sought to strengthen the banking sector and to revive business. Government make-work programs were tried so that workers would not have to go on the dole. When public support was the only resort, the federal government stepped in to undergird the faltering state and local programs.

Some of the New Deal initiatives were intended to be temporary and went away when the economy revived as World War II began. Other programs, like Social Security, were meant to provide a permanent solution to economic vulnerability. One minor program of federal assistance to widows who had children to support—later called Aid to Families with Dependent Children—expanded and became the core of American public welfare.

President Roosevelt hoped that his New Deal would not create dependency. When a household lost its breadwinner through widowhood, illness, accidents, or old age, it was right to have a program to ensure economic security. The other support programs were designed to restore people to work while upholding them in the meantime, and were never meant to make them dependent on a soul-chilling handout. These were good goals, and no doubt the great crisis demanded great new initiatives even if there was reason, then and later, to wonder about the size and effectiveness of the New Deal social effort.

There was a very troubling side effect, however, to the New Deal's expanded government role. The balance between private and public was reversed. The very first regulation of the New Deal program that was set up to give federal cash assistance to the poor through state and local government offices insisted that only government officials could handle government funds. So the hundreds of private agencies that partnered with state and local authorities would have to be excluded unless they agreed to be deputized as government agents. The Social Security Act accelerated the change in balance.[6]

Private and religious programs did not disappear, of course, but the center of gravity for social assistance was displaced. Government became the major initiator and provider of services. Even though the new programs often involved all three levels of government—federal, state, and local—the federal government was the dominating force. The help Americans gave to other Americans would no longer primarily be the result of what local groups, religious and secular, designed and provided. Government would be the center, and if government was to be the center, then religion would be on the margin.

This new pattern was maintained as federal programs were added and expanded after World War II. The emphasis on government and secularism was especially strong in the 1960s with President Lyndon Johnson's Great Society and War on Poverty. Even when, later in the 1960s, the government began increasingly to turn to nongovernmental organizations to deliver the social services that lawmakers had decided should be offered, the watchwords were *government* and *secularism.*

That was a sad irony. By the 1980s, a majority of government-funded social services were actually delivered not by government staff but instead by private groups—secular nonprofits, businesses, religiously affiliated nonprofit organizations.[7] But officials thought of these private groups not as partners but as vendors or contractors. Officials sought private agencies that would do what government wanted; they weren't spending their time looking for the best private efforts to support with government funds. In this system, religious groups might be able to take part, but their religion was supposed to be left behind.

NOT A SINGLE DOLLAR OF TAXPAYER MONEY FOR RELIGION

Why was the system so secular even when religious groups were playing such a key role? It wasn't just because government had taken the dominant position. Rather, at the same time as the new patterns of social services were being developed, ideas about the right relationship between church and state were changing.[8]

The United States Constitution, of course, requires government to respect the religious liberty of all its citizens. One way it must show that respect is by refusing to single out some particular church or faith for governmental favor as an established religion. Church and state have to be separate so that government can do justice to all rather than showing partiality to some. Meanwhile, churches are not to bend to the will of the powers of the day. However, separating church and state does not require pushing all faith out of public affairs and activities. As we have seen, early on in American history state and local officials routinely joined with religious (as well as secular) groups to aid people in need.

Despite historic precedents, maintaining the right relationship between religion and public affairs became more complex as the United States became more religiously diverse. When most Americans were Protestant, they expected, rather than objected to, a Christian tint to public life. Yet it was obvious to the Catholic immigrants who arrived in large numbers later in the nineteenth century that the "nonsectarian" faith that infused government-funded schools and welfare services was not the Catholic version of Christianity. Jewish citizens also objected to the Christian veneer, and so did immigrants who came with yet other religions, along with Americans who rejected all traditional faiths. The informal establishment of Protestantism had to go, but what should government do about religion if it could not maintain this collaboration with a generalized Christian faith?

The United States Supreme Court's solution was what came to be called "no-aid separationism"—nothing the government does or supports can be religious. That way the government can avoid taking sides; it can avoid establishing religion.

The new guideline was announced in ringing tones for the Court by Justice Hugo Black in the 1947 case, *Everson v. Board of Education.* The Constitution's requirement of no establishment of religion, Justice Black wrote, means that neither the federal government nor a state government can organize a church. It also means that the governments are forbidden to adopt laws that favor one or another religion, or religion over secularism. Justice Black also insisted that the no-establishment requirement also means that "no tax in any amount, large or small, can be levied to support any religious activities or institutions, whatever they may be called, or whatever form they may adopt to teach or practice religion."[9]

There it was: No-aid separationism. Government cannot support religion, religious teachings, or religious activities. So if officials want to buy drug treatment or homeless services from a nongovernmental provider instead of hiring government employees to offer the help, then obviously religious providers are ineligible to be considered.

Yet maybe they are eligible after all. For, despite Justice Black's emphatic words, he was part of a Court majority that ruled in the case that it was constitutionally permissible for the State of New Jersey to use state taxpayers' money to subsidize students' bus rides to parochial schools. No tax money to support religion was the declaration, but tax money that in a way supported religious schooling was approved in the decision. So maybe government could collaborate with religion after all. In short, although Justice Black's declaration was crystal clear, the actual position of the Court on church-state collaboration was not so clear.[10]

Over the next decades, the Court tried out various formulas or tests to mark out a bright line between permitted and unconstitutional cooperation. Nothing was very convincing. Instead of clarity there was arbitrariness. As the late New York Democratic Senator Daniel Patrick Moynihan once famously asked, if the Supreme Court thought it was constitutional for a state to supply books to parochial schools but not maps, whatever would it do about atlases—books of maps?

If the details were fuzzy, the big message was obvious enough. The informal establishment of Protestantism would have to give way to what Richard John Neuhaus picturesquely called "the naked public square." If government touched an activity, that activity should be devoid of religion. If government funded the activity, it should not have any religion in it. After all, in a religiously diverse society, how could the government avoid taking sides unless it avoided supporting religion entirely? Officials could treat all faiths fairly only by equally excluding all of them from whatever government did or supported.

Yet this formula did not fit reality well—not at all. Federal, state, and local officials often decided they wanted to support the social services provided by religiously affiliated groups, just as New Jersey decided it was good policy to subsidize bus transportation to parochial schools. Lutheran Services of America, Catholic Charities, the Salvation Army, and various Jewish organizations are only the most prominent religious social service organizations that over the years have received hundreds of thousands, even millions of dollars to support their assistance programs.

Religiously affiliated groups are part of the mix of nongovernmental providers through which our governments offer assistance to the poor and needy. However, although the no-aid doctrine did not prevent this extensive relationship from developing, it did ensure that the relationship would be a troubled one. The terms used to name the religious providers already tells the story. These days such providers are called "faith-based organizations," but that name reflects a changed relationship between government and religious organizations. Until the recent changes in that relationship, the government's religious partners were commonly called "religiously affiliated" or "religion-sponsored" organizations. Service organizations that received government money could have a faith or church connection, but religion was supposed to be kept far away from the services government supported and authorized.

This unhappy formula created arbitrary funding decisions, insecurity, pressures to secularize, and even game playing. A religious provider might be required to remove or hide religious signs and symbols as the price of getting government funds. Worse, religious organizations that sought government support often had to promise not to ask potential employees about their faith commitments.

Sometimes the pressure was about names: in the Southwest, city officials once tried to force the St. Vincent de Paul Society to become the Mr. Vincent de Paul Society. In a Northeast city, other officials blustered that the Salvation Army would have to change the first part of its name if it wanted to march with the city. In the 1980s lawyers in the federal Department of Housing and Urban Development released funding for groups with religious mission statements only after the lawyers assured themselves that the "God talk" no longer meant anything. The Heritage Foundation's Joe Loconte once wrote that these kinds of requirements amounted to government "seducing the Samaritan."[11] Or, in the words of constitutional law scholar Michael McConnell, such anti-faith requirements made government grant programs "relentless engines of secularization."[12]

Certainly not all Samaritans who have accepted government money have been seduced. The Salvation Army, for one, has labored long and creatively to preserve its gospel character and to offer spiritual as well as material care, despite the restrictive conditions that government officials (and sometimes corporate donors) want to attach to the funds. In fact, often government's antireligious bark is much worse than its bite. Stephen Monsma's early 1990s survey of religiously affiliated child service agencies showed that, even though a majority received some or much government money, almost all included religious activities such as talking about faith with the kids and families, praying over meals, or displaying religious pictures.[13]

Yet all the good news, as Monsma pointed out, was not good enough. The rules are inconsistent between one program and another, one bureaucrat and another, one year and the next. As long as the legal foundations are shaky and no-aid separationism is the constitutional doctrine, such partnerships are at risk. An official's visit to a religious provider to highlight the excellent work it does in partnership with government might be just the trigger for a lawsuit claiming the partnership is illegal and unconstitutional.

That is what happened when Republican presidential candidate George W. Bush visited FaithWorks Milwaukee, an evangelical residential drug treatment program. Almost immediately the Freedom from Religion Foundation sued the State of Wisconsin, claiming the partnership was unconstitutional. (The court in fact ruled that part of the contract was improperly designed but the partnership otherwise was perfectly legal.) Government practice might be flexible and often positive, but without a secure legal and constitutional foundation, a religious group that chooses to accept government funds always has to worry that one day it might be struck by lightning.

ENDING WELFARE AS WE KNOW IT

By the start of the 1990s, our welfare system, and other social services, too, had few enthusiastic defenders. The federal, state, and local governments were spending billions of dollars each year and either operated or contracted for hundreds of different programs to respond to one kind of need or another. There had always been complaints about how expensive all this was, but now the real concern was deeper, shared by more and more observers. Whether you worried about wasteful programs or about the single moms who remained trapped in poverty, the drug addicts who didn't recover, or the teens who went down the wrong path without ever meeting a rescuer, somehow all that spending and all those programs didn't seem to be doing very much good. Too often the programs seemed even to promote bad choices and values instead of instilling the ability to make good ones.

In the case of welfare, many thought that what President Roosevelt had warned against had come true. Welfare had become a handout instead of a hand up. Despite various reforms, including a major change in 1988, the system did not seem to require or help people to become independent. That wasn't just a conservative complaint. President Bill Clinton's welfare advisers wrote that the very definition of public welfare had become the welfare office, where government workers spent their time not trying to help families achieve self-sufficiency but rather carefully calculating the size of the government checks the families could claim. Welfare mothers who made progress by finding part-time work or a temporary job actually messed up the system by necessitating that their eligibility for a check be calculated again and again.[14]

This was not the way to help people who had to count on the help of others. Bill Clinton, running for president in 1992 as a New Democrat, brought the issue to a head by calling for an "end to welfare as we know it." Many states were also anxious for change, and some had already won exemptions from various federal rules so they could experiment with better ways to help the needy. Congress was also ready for a change. At the start there wasn't a lot of agreement on just how the system could be improved, but few in Congress were satisfied any longer with simply demanding more or less welfare.

In August 1996 President Clinton signed the federal welfare reform bill, giving the nation's welfare system a new direction and stimulating similar changes in other social programs. The new law, the Personal Responsibility and Work Opportunity Reconciliation Act, made three big changes.[15]

- First, after six decades of taking more and more control of government welfare into its own hands, Congress announced a reversal of course. Although the federal government would continue to pay for about half of the welfare bill, it was once again the job of state and local authorities to figure out just what the welfare needs were in their areas and to come up with their own plans for addressing those needs.
- Second, the emphasis of welfare was changed from paying checks to the poor to providing help so they could become independent—able to support themselves and give to others.

Aid to Families with Dependent Children became Temporary Assistance for Needy Families. Poor families would receive income support but also services and encouragement to make the transition from welfare to work.

• Third, welfare was released from its dominance by government to become (again) a partnership with charities and businesses. At last it was recognized that officials could hardly expect families to become independent if businesses and social groups were left out of the picture. Bridges to society had to be built. People needed the kind of help that government could not deliver on its own: life and job skills; a personal connection into the job market; wisdom about managing work, home, and family; a mentor or job coach; and a supportive network.

The goal of empowerment and independence for the underprivileged pressed state and local welfare officials to discover and develop relationships with businesses, community groups, and faith-based organizations, but Congress didn't just give general encouragement for partnerships. The 1996 federal welfare reform law included a short section on partnerships, which came to be called "Charitable Choice." This section of the law actually *required* state and local officials to welcome as full partners religious organizations that they had often been excluding.

A NEWER DEAL: INVITING RELIGION BACK IN

How did such a clause find its way into federal law? The "special partnership" language of the welfare reform law was the fruit of a dramatic new view of religious charities as part of our social safety net—an appropriate and necessary role. Instead of religion being marginalized in a government-dominated system, officials and social workers would have to acknowledge the vital services provided by religious organizations and work in partnership with them. In the words of Ram Cnaan, University of Pennsylvania social work professor, it was past time to exchange the New Deal for a "Newer Deal."[16] Many voices by the 1990s were declaring that faith-based programs had to be brought back to the forefront in the fight against our society's many social problems.

Political leaders, editorial writers, and even academics now said that conventional social services are just too shallow to help people overcome their most pressing problems. William Raspberry, columnist for the *Washington Post*, wrote, "I have seen lives turned around—sometimes almost miraculously. Seldom, though, has the agent of that change been a government program. . . . Most often profound change begins on the inside and then transforms every-thing else. I'm talking about spiritual change, whether specifically religious or not." If that was the case, Raspberry went on, then it was time to figure out "how to combine the efforts of government with those of faith-based organizations" in order to "create the sort of change we need." If the ACLU complained about such partner-ships, he said, that was just too bad.[17]

Similarly, in an article entitled "In God They Trust," published in the *New Yorker*, Joe Klein quoted a Clinton administration White House aide as saying that the idea of expanding the role of faith-based groups "certainly seems to be the hot social-policy topic these days," and the late liberal Democratic Senator Paul Wellstone (Minnesota) as saying, "Some of the best antipoverty work I've seen has come from faith-based agencies."[18]

There was another major reason why many were looking for a Newer Deal. A phrase from Marvin Olasky points to it. The main problem with welfare, he once said, was not that it was too expensive but that it was too cheap. Welfare is a stingy response to need. All that it asks of us is tax money, when what we should give are acts of compassion and service. That's what a person in distress needs—hands-on human assistance—and it is also what we should readily offer.

Not only Christian activists were calling for a revival of per-sonal compassion and generosity. Remember President Ronald Reagan's challenge to people to get personally involved and not always look to government for solutions? Remember President George H. W. Bush's Thousand Points of Light? For more than two decades Americans have been repeatedly reminding each other of our heritage of citizen activism. This is the legacy of neighbors joining together to help their neighbors that Alexis de Tocqueville had so long ago identified as a characteristically American way of responding to problems.[19]

Interestingly, it wasn't just Americans who were feeling that turning responsibility over to government had gone too far. Think of the challenge that citizen groups, faith leaders, and independent associations mounted in the 1980s against totalitarianism in the Eastern Block, bringing down Eastern and Central European tyrants, the Berlin Wall, and even the once-mighty Soviet Union. Without so much drama but more widely, government officials, policy experts, and scholars in many Western countries and around the globe throughout the 1990s were suggesting that government had become too big, at the expense of social groups and volunteers.

Government has many strengths, but its programs are complex, slow, and one-size-fits-all, and they touch people only externally. Meanwhile, many social problems involve the heart and conscience and require an individualized approach. Whatever the best size for government, somehow secular grassroots groups and faith-based organizations had to play larger roles in solving social problems.

A major study of "The Emerging Nonprofit Sector," published in 1996, pointed out that "a major reappraisal" of the role of government was under way "throughout the world—in the developed countries of North America, Europe, and Asia; in the developing societies of Asia, Africa, and Latin America; and in the former Soviet bloc." Government programs are too costly and not very effective, so people around the globe were looking for new solutions that relied more on nonprofit organizations.[20]

In the national and international ferment, all kinds of ideas were suggested. One of the most creative plans was the Project for American Renewal, proposed in 1995 by Dan Coats, then a Republican senator from Indiana and currently U.S. ambassador to Germany. Government was standing in the way of citizens' good works, Coats said, encouraging us to think that we didn't need to care for our neighbors because the government would do it for us. That had to stop, but it wasn't likely that we would all suddenly become active merely because government stepped aside.

Coats offered more than a dozen ways that the government could encourage us to take back more responsibility for caring for others. For example, the federal government could extend its malpractice insurance to cover doctors and nurses willing to serve the poor without charge. Government could give vouchers to expectant single moms so they could afford to choose a maternal group home run by caring folks. School districts could get federal demonstration grants to work with community and faith groups to develop mentoring programs for their students.

At the center of his project Coats proposed a charity tax credit. Taxpayers should get an actual credit against their federal taxes for contributions they made to poverty-fighting charities. Then the federal treasury would take in less, so the federal budget for welfare and social services would shrink, but, in turn, citizens would be directly investing their money in private groups they trusted to effectively assist the poor, the homeless, and the hungry.

Government action would stimulate, not discourage, a greater flourishing of secular and religious social outreach. The late Democratic Senator Daniel Patrick Moynihan, who for two decades had been Congress's leading expert on social services, exclaimed that Senator Coats's ideas were "the most compelling and thoughtful" he had heard on these problems in all those years.[21]

Another ground-breaking idea also was proposed as a way to bring faith back more fully into the social safety net. This idea involved the services government itself paid for. Helping charities to flourish was an excellent plan, but many government programs would still be there. Often people in need had to turn to government programs because they were either the only services available or the only services with space for new clients.

And sometimes people needing help had no choice of where to go. When a judge said, "Get help or go to jail!" or a caseworker said, "Enroll in job training or you'll lose your welfare check," the government expected the person to go to a program that it supported and supervised. Was there a way to get more faith-based services into this network? Could government contracts and grants be made more friendly to groups that took their faith so seriously that they insisted on being faith-based and not only religiously affiliated?

Fortunately, in a string of cases that started early in the 1980s, the Supreme Court was changing its own thinking about such partnerships. No-aid separationism was on its way out. In its place, the Court began adopting a new doctrine: government neutrality or equal treatment. No-aid separationism told government to try to be fair to all faiths by excluding them all from government support. The result was discrimination against faith-based programs and organizations as the government, in effect, became an evangelist for secular views and programs.

The new "equal treatment" strategy instead required government to be evenhanded. If public high schools allowed students
to organize clubs after school, then the schools could no longer
forbid religious clubs (the 1984 Equal Access Act, upheld by the
U.S. Supreme Court in *Board of Education v. Mergens*, 1990). Since the
University of Virginia used student fees to underwrite the printing
of other student newspapers, it would have to stop its discriminatory practice of withholding support just from the evangelical paper
(U.S. Supreme Court case, *Rosenberger v. Rector*, 1995). Congress had
been following, not ignoring, the Constitution when it invited religious groups, along with others, to sponsor abstinence-education
training (U.S. Supreme Court case, *Bowen v. Kendrick*, 1988). Reli-
gious-school students entitled to federally funded remedial help
could receive it from public school teachers right in their religious
schools and did not have to first walk to a secular property (U.S.
Supreme Court case, *Agostini v. Felton*, 1997, reversing its own 1985
decisions), and so on.[22]

If equal treatment was the right way to interpret the First
Amendment's twin requirements to promote religious liberty
while avoiding establishment of religion, then it was time for a
new guideline for government funding of social services provided
by other organizations. It could not be right to exclude religious
providers simply because they were religious or to require them
to become as nonreligious as possible as the price of accepting
government funds. Equal treatment required that they have an
equal opportunity to become government's partners in a renewed
and more intensive fight against social ills. Equal treatment for
faith-based providers is the partnership innovation that Congress
initiated in the 1996 federal welfare reform law by including the
Charitable Choice provision.

CHARITABLE CHOICE: BRINGING RELIGION BACK IN

This Newer Deal, in which government partners more extensively
with faith-based organizations that work with distressed families
and communities, required more than an enthusiastic invitation
from government officials to America's faith communities. Faith-
based organizations needed not only a warm welcome but a more

Service That Respects Other Peoples' Faiths

It is a snowy February morning in Philadelphia and dozens of men and women, bundled up against the cold, are filing into a large brick building on the corner of Twelfth and Lehigh. For decades Cookman United Methodist Church has been the centerpiece of this impoverished neighborhood. Each Sunday its walls resonate with the sounds of hundreds of voices worshiping together. Today, however, the folks entering Cookman, blowing on their cold hands and shaking the snow off their caps, have come to attend a weekly computer literacy class taught by members of the church staff. The class is part of Cookman's Transitional Journey program, a faith-centered social service course that is funded by the federal government through the Pennsylvania Department of Public Welfare.

Today is Josephine Campbell's third day at Cookman. Josephine is a single mother whose husband was jailed over two years ago for drug possession with intent to deal. She has been on welfare since last July when she was laid off from her job at a local meat packing plant. Josephine has had difficulty finding work but wants desperately to provide a better life for her four-year-old daughter. She has dreams of moving to a safer neighborhood someday and of standing on her own two feet without food stamps or government checks. She hopes Cookman can provide her with the skills that will help her to realize her dreams.

Mary Stevens watches the chilly, damp group make their way into the building. She has just begun her twelfth year as a full-time member of the Cookman staff. She has been a part of dozens of community programs, but none of them has been as unique or as challenging as Transitional Journey, which is a pioneering program showing how Pennsylvania welfare officials are partnering with faith-based organizations that in the past were ignored.

When Transitional Journey was in its infancy, Stevens and her colleagues knew it was perfectly acceptable under new guidelines that the program could be clearly faith-based, but they were unsure about the extent to which explicitly religious practices such as prayer and Bible reading could be offered to program participants. The Charitable Choice provision of the federal welfare reform law said that faith-based programs like Transitional Journey were eligible to get federal funding through state authorities, but it also carefully protected the religious liberty of clients and emphasized that the purpose of welfare spending is to help families become independent, not to underwrite evangelism or church expansion. So just how did these various freedoms and duties fit together? Pennsylvania officials weren't so sure at the start, and neither were Transitional Journey staffers.

Initially, the staff used the Bible as the program's primary reading source and did not offer any alternative activities to clients who objected to participating in explicitly religious activities. State officials monitoring

respectful environment. They needed government to change its funding rules to respect, rather than encroach upon, their religious character. It was just such a change in rules, and not only a warmer welcome, that the Charitable Choice provision offered.[23]

the program informed Mary that the federally funded job-preparation program could not require anyone to take part in worship or discipleship activities.

It was a difficult time for Mary, Cookman's pastor, Reverend Donna Jones, and the rest of the staff. Were the government's rules reasonable, or did they go too far? What was the right way for a faith-filled program to serve someone who valued the program's job training and life-skills classes but didn't want to take part in religious activities—maybe because she belonged to a different denomination, or a different faith, or rejected faith altogether?

In Mary's own words:

Every worker that did this program is a born again believer. It has strengthened all of the workers. We know that there are things we have to do that we do not like doing. We ask the Lord to guide us in such a way that it will still come down as the best thing for the situation, from a Christian perspective. And we got challenged on the things that we do. Even though it was clear in the proposal that this would be run as a Christian organization, we were challenged by the state in some of the things we were doing, because someone took offense that we used the Bible as reading material. We had to change that around and offer alternative material. People did become offended that we had services on Friday, so we had to offer alternative time if they did not want to go to the service. But we still persevered.

The Cookman staff, including Mary, has worked hard to cooperate with the government's guidelines. Of course, the staff wants to witness to the "hope that is within them" and to share the Christian gospel with everyone who hasn't heard it. Yet salvation is a free gift, and belief must be the choice of a willing heart. No one wants to try to coerce anyone into accepting Christianity. So the staff modified the Transitional Journey program to make it clear that, while everyone is invited to join in the spiritual activities, no participant is required to do so.

Mary takes note of Josephine as she pulls off her second-hand parka and bright pink muffler and settles eagerly in front of an available computer terminal. She knows Josephine does not consider herself to be a Christian. But in their conversations, she's learned that the young mother feels there is, somehow, a different attitude around Cookman. In her words, "I've been to other places and stayed for a while, but there was always a spirit of anger. People's attitudes were demoralizing there."

Josephine has assured Mary that she plans to stick with the Transitional Journey program. "I like it here. I like the way people make me feel—like they really love me. I'd like to know more about why they are so different. And hopefully the skills I learn here will help me to find a job and start life again."[24]

John Ashcroft, then a Republican senator from Missouri, now attorney general in the Bush administration, put Charitable Choice into the welfare law. The basic idea came from Carl Esbeck, a law professor in Missouri who had worked extensively on First Amendment issues and with evangelical social service groups. For a book project, Esbeck had completed an extensive analysis of federal, state, and local rules that unconstitutionally restrict faith-based groups. Not satisfied with only pointing out the problems, he drafted legal language to overturn the excessive restrictions, in line with the Court's new idea of equal treatment.

Esbeck's remedy for government restrictions on faith-based social services was the main feature of a short welfare reform bill that Senator Ashcroft proposed in 1995. Senator Ashcroft then worked to include that remedy in the welfare bill that Congress passed and President Clinton signed in the summer of 1996. Charitable Choice laid down a new guideline for state officials to follow when they used federal government funds to obtain welfare services. The aim of the new guideline, according to the language of the law, was to make it possible for states to choose faith-based providers "on the same basis as any other nongovernmental provider" without "impairing the religious character" of those providers or "diminishing the religious freedom" of people seeking the welfare help.[25]

There would be no more pressure on religious providers to conceal their faith, no more exclusion of faith-based providers that looked too religious to a government official—or that a government official feared might look too religious to groups that fight against religious liberty. In short, there was to be equal treatment of religious and secular groups that compete for government funding for their services, respect for the religious character of religious providers, and protection for the religious liberty of recipients of help.

Charitable Choice was a federal rule or condition, a string that followed federal welfare money out to state governments. It was a new rule for state officials to follow when they searched to purchase effective services that could help families move from welfare to independence. As Amy Sherman pointed out, it gave a green light to building new partnerships between government and faith-based organizations. To government officials and to leaders of faith-based organizations it said, "Washington has given its blessing" to expanded collaboration.[26] It signaled a new era of partnerships and highlighted the Supreme Court's changed doctrine on church and state relations.

Charitable Choice was not only a green light for new partnerships, it was also a new framework for such partnerships. It provided new rules in one of the most restrictive areas of government policy—government expenditure of taxpayer money to buy help for vulnerable people.

Charitable Choice can be summarized in four points:

- It requires government officials not to discriminate against churches and faith-based nonprofits when deciding which organization can receive grants or contracts to provide social services.
- It obligates the government to respect the religious character of faith-based providers that accept government money by protecting the providers' right to maintain a religious environment and to select staff on a religious basis.
- It protects the religious liberty of people needing help by ensuring that they will be helped without religious discrimination and are not coerced into religious observance, and by requiring government to provide an alternative to people who do not want to be served by a faith-based provider.
- It fulfills constitutional guidelines by requiring that government funds be used to provide welfare services and not be diverted to support inherently religious activities such as evangelization and worship.

The Charitable Choice standard is not perfect. The courts are not yet fully free of the old no-aid separationism idea, so there is a limit to how innovative the law can become and still withstand court challenges. Yet Charitable Choice firmly protects the religious character of faith-based organizations and their freedom to offer their own evangelism and discipleship training next to government-funded programs of social service.

Adopted as part of the 1996 welfare law, Charitable Choice was the guideline for state and local governments deciding how to spend their federal welfare (TANF) funds. A year later, Congress created a short-term Welfare-to-Work program to give special help to families facing a particularly difficult transition off welfare. Enacted as an amendment to the 1996 welfare law, this new program's spending also came under the Charitable Choice guideline.

In 1998 Congress reauthorized the Community Services Block Grant (CSBG) program, which provides basic federal funding for

Community Action Agencies that provide a range of services in poor neighborhoods. As part of that reauthorization, Congress added the Charitable Choice guideline, so that when Community Action Agencies use those CSBG funds to buy services, faith-based providers are eligible to take part.

Then in 2000 Congress added the Charitable Choice guidelines to federal drug treatment funds administered by the Substance Abuse and Mental Health Services Administration (SAMHSA)— money used by federal, state, and local officials to support programs for drug addicts.

Interview on 9 December 2002 with Tony Campolo, professor emeritus of sociology, Eastern College; founder of the Evangelical Association for the Promotion of Education; widely known Christian speaker and author

---

Q: Some people seem to think that the faith-based initiative began with the election of George W. Bush as president. Yet some of the key first steps occurred during the Clinton presidency. How do you see the background of the current effort to expand government partnerships with faith-based groups?

A: The person who initiated the faith-based approach was not Bush but Clinton. He received some criticism, but moderate Democrats endorse this for the simple reason that the problems we face as a society are so great that government cannot do it alone nor can the faith-based sector do it alone. Some form of cooperation is essential.

Faith-based programs are great not just because they are efficient with money but because they have an incredible capacity for creating volunteerism. If you look at the great American experience of volunteerism, the reality is that the churches supply most of the volunteers. The majority of the work we do in our program is done by people who get no pay at all. Obviously this is a bonanza for a community. If the government had to pay for the services that are being rendered by faith-based organizations, it could never meet the needs of society. The faith-based organizations have people but no money; the government has money but not enough people. So can we work together and contribute to each other? That became Clinton's argument, which won a following within the Democratic Party. Insofar as the Democratic Party allows the faith-based initiative to become a conservative Republican agenda, the Democrats will lose the American people. The American people are solidly behind this—there is overwhelming support.

The federal government, it was clear, was seeking new partnerships with faith-based organizations. Congress had realized that the government had to redesign the rules that had made collaboration with government a risky venture for faith-based organizations. So, across a range of federal programs, the legal rules had been changed.

The stage was set for a new engagement between government and faith-based social services, but many questions remained:

- Would the federal government and state and local officials actually change the way they spent their government funds to obtain services?
- Did the new rules provide sufficient protection for faith-based organizations?
- Was it wise for a religious group to seek government funds, or should it rely instead on faithful believers?
- If faith-based providers joined with government, would that improve the government-funded services or, instead, drag down the faith-based providers to the level of inefficient and ineffective government services?

There were—and are—plenty of challenges demanding care and prayer, and we will discuss some of those challenges in the pages that follow. Yet the foundation has been laid: Between 1996 and 2000, Congress created a new framework for partnership between government and faith-based organizations. This framework, we believe, challenges faith leaders to consider—carefully and prayerfully—just how their service to others, their commitment to "love our neighbor," should relate to the nation's social safety net.

3

A New Partnership

I believe strongly in the separation of church and state.
But freedom of religion need not mean freedom from reli-
gion. There is a better way.

Former Vice President Al Gore

One of George W. Bush's first major actions when
he became president of the United States in January
2001 was to announce that his new administration would promote legislative and administrative change to expand the federal
government's partnerships with faith-based organizations and
with grassroots groups. The response was a storm of congressional
opposition, which implied that he had proposed an outlandish and
unprecedented idea. This public criticism came not only from the
usual antireligious voices but also from faith leaders who feared the
undermining of Christian ministries.

In reality, however, the movement to invite faith-based social services
back into the center of the nation's fight against poverty is thriving.
After all, it began before the Bush administration, and the idea had
received bipartisan support, including a strong endorsement from
Bush's Democratic rival for the presidency, former Vice President Al
Gore.

A Clarion Call for a New Partnership

It is 1999, and the Democratic and Republican primary campaigns for president of the United States are heating up. Hundreds stand waiting, their faces rapt in anticipation. Some are holding signs displaying messages of encouragement and support, while others wave small American flags high in the air. The words, "Strengthening Faith and Family" are projected in bold black letters onto a screen behind the empty stage.

Excitement ripples across the room as a man takes his place center stage. The crowd comes alive when he stands at the podium and looks across a sea of waving flags and clapping hands. The din of cheers, whistles, and chanted phrases is deafening. The man smiles and waves, basking in the warm welcome. Eventually he motions for the crowd to settle and waits for a hush to fall before he begins to speak.

"I want to talk today about a dramatic transformation in America. It's one that you and your families are already a part of. This transformation is a quiet one—and a good one. It is a movement that is entirely about solutions. And it is sweeping from home to home and neighbor to neighbor, right now in America."

The crowd listens intently as the man speaks of the importance of religion in one's daily life and of a grassroots movement of Americans reaching out to their hurting neighbors instead of waiting for government to act. They listen as he calls for "a new partnership" between government and faith-based organizations.

What we need, the presidential candidate says, is to expand Charitable Choice beyond

Despite the opposition, under President Bush federal programs are being redesigned to be faith-friendly. In response to the Charitable Choice rules adopted into law under the Clinton administration, states and local governments are increasingly reaching out to faith-based programs to provide effective help to the needy. At all levels of government, policies and practices are being changed from hostility to hospitality, creating a level playing field that makes it possible for faith-based groups to decide for themselves whether their mission of service to the hurting will be more fruitful if they grasp government's outstretched hand. Let's take a closer look at how this began and how it continues.

RALLYING THE ARMIES OF COMPASSION

President Bush launched his initiative on 29 January 2001. This took place at the start of the second week of his administration, first in a private meeting with ministry and nonprofit leaders, and then before the press in the historic Indian Treaty Room in the welfare services to other areas such as drug treatment, homelessness, and prevention of youth violence. As long as people who seek help can find a secular alternative and aren't forced into religious practices, he says, faith-based organizations should be welcomed to provide such services with government funds "and without having to alter the religious character that is so often the key to their effectiveness." He challenges the audience: "We must dare to embrace faith-based approaches that advance our shared goals as Americans" because "faith in itself is sometimes essential to spark a personal transformation, and to keep that person from falling back into addiction, delinquency, or dependency."

Is the man speaking George W. Bush, the Republican presidential candidate? These are views that Americans have certainly come to expect at a conservative political gathering. They have, by now, accepted such ideas as part of George W. Bush's vision for America.

But no, this isn't Bush. This was Democratic presidential candidate Al Gore, who delivered this speech at the Salvation Army's Adult Rehabilitation Center in Atlanta on 24 May 1999. Ever since Republican Senator John D. Ashcroft added the Charitable Choice provision to President Clinton's 1996 welfare reform legislation, the idea of governmental support of faith-based organizations has been gaining bipartisan support. Growing numbers of policy makers are coming to believe that cooperation between church and state to serve the poor and needy is an important innovation that must be allowed to flourish.[1]

Old Executive Office Building, next door to the White House. In his speech and in the booklet released to the press, "Rallying the Armies of Compassion," the president pointed out that, although America is a land of prosperity and promise, many Americans suffer from poverty, drugs, family breakdown, homelessness, or violence. Despite many government programs and much spending, the help offered has often not been very effective.[2]

To make a lasting change, President Bush said, we must turn to our "neighborhood healers"—grassroots groups, charities, faith-based programs. "These quiet heroes lift people's lives in ways that are beyond government's know-how, usually on shoestring budgets, and they heal our nation's ills one heart and one act of kindness at a time." Such "armies of compassion" must no longer be neglected but instead be honored and supported, and when the federal government seeks partners to provide welfare and social services, it must include these faith-based and community groups.

Government has its own vital role to play, President Bush emphasized, and secular and religiously affiliated nonprofit social services have traditionally been its valued partners. He explained that we need to enlarge the network by ending the federal neglect of faith-based and grassroots groups—groups that often provide critically important and effective help to distressed families and communities. The president called for a bold new federal social policy that would respond to "the growing consensus across America that successful government social programs work in fruitful partnership with community-serving and faith-based organizations." He vowed that the Bush administration would dedicate itself to "enlist, equip, enable, empower, and expand the heroic works of faith-based and community groups across America."

"Starting now," the president proclaimed, "the federal government is adopting a new attitude to honor and not restrict faith-based and community initiatives, to accept rather than dismiss such programs, and to empower rather than ignore them." He issued an executive order creating a new White House Office of Faith-Based and Community Initiatives as the lead federal agency to promote the new policy to support and enlist the neglected armies of compassion.

In a second executive order, President Bush established counterpart Centers for Faith-Based and Community Initiatives in five federal departments that extensively fund social services: Health and Human Services (HHS), Housing and Urban Development (HUD), Education, Justice, and Labor. A similar taskforce was created at the Corporation for National and Community Service, which runs AmeriCorps, VISTA, the Peace Corps, and other federal volunteerism initiatives. An executive order issued in December 2002 also established Centers in the Department of Agriculture and in the Agency for International Development.

A HUE AND CRY

Unquestionably, President Bush's idea that somehow public social programs need to connect with faith-based groups and with the transformative power of faith was a popular one. A few years before, in 1999, the Democratic Leadership Council (composed of centrist or moderate Democrats) had asked people whom they thought could best address social problems. Eight percent thought government was best; 16 percent believed that religious and charitable groups, independent of government, were best; but nearly three-quarters of those surveyed—72 percent (77 percent of Democrats, 60 percent of Republicans)—said that a closer collaboration between government and religious and charitable groups was the best solution. In early January 2001, as the Bush administration was being formed, a new survey confirmed those views, showing that more than six out of ten people surveyed favored government funding of church and parachurch programs for the poor.[3]

Of course, views about how best to build new partnerships continue to differ, but what the president was proposing was, at its heart, simply to translate the broad consensus into revised government practices, accelerating the changes that had started during the Clinton administration. President Bush did advocate the sensitive idea of increasing federal funding of faith-based programs, but one of his major aims was to multiply individual and corporate donations to secular and religious charities. When it came to federal collaboration, he clearly was not planning an unconstitutional theocratic welfare state. He called for equal opportunity, for the government to partner with all effective programs, "whether run by Methodists, Muslims, Mormons, or good people of no faith at all."[4] The goal was effective help and a level playing field.

Yet who could guess any of that from listening to the critics? Charitable Choice had been adopted into law multiple times during the previous administration and had bipartisan support during the presidential campaign. Despite all that, a bill to expand the principle to additional federal programs—the Community Solutions Act, cosponsored by Democrat Tony Hall (Ohio) and Republican J. C. Watts (Oklahoma)—barely passed the House and was declared dead on arrival when it was sent for Senate action.

The Senate's watered-down substitute was the CARE Act, which emphasized increased private giving to overcome declining donations in the wake of 9/11 and the economic downturn but included only minor innovations to promote partnerships. Despite broad bipartisan cosponsorship and the support of more than sixteen hundred nonprofit groups, the bill languished for months, held hostage by anti-faith forces. Some senators actually tried to add to it language to put new restrictions on faith-based groups. The 107th Congress ended in November 2002 without the Senate even voting on its version of faith-based legislation.

Q: You know that some African-American religious and secular leaders have been suspicious of the president's faith-based initiative, seeing it mainly as a Republican ploy to gain black votes. Do black religious leaders remain suspicious?

A: There's been a change of awareness, and people are becoming a little more comfortable with the president's goals. I commend President Bush for his efforts and for being able to stand and take the heat of criticism about his actions and motives. But at the same time, Democrats, with whom most blacks identify, are very aware that his initiative and administration are Republican. So there is a political aspect. Besides that, with a Republican administration, black leaders don't have the same easy access as they had before. So there's been some hesitancy about trying to get involved.

Black leaders who are interested have to find new ways of making contact. During the Clinton administration black leaders knew just how to get into the system. One phone call and we could get into the White House.

Things changed on 9/11. The president's agenda has been so full in relation to homeland security and all that he has not been able to reach out to the black community as he would like to, even though he has continued to advocate his faith-based initiative.

But I don't think his initiative is a tool to gain black votes. I had the opportunity to sit and talk with President Bush when he was running for office. He has very deep religious convictions. I just personally feel those are part of the man. He knows that the church has been very effective in changing communities—more effective than government. So why waste money by ignoring faith-based services?

Beyond Capitol Hill, critics from all sides blasted the Bush initiatives as unwise, unconstitutional, or un-Christian. Many of the opponents simply were determined to keep religion confined to private life. Others were rank partisans, determined to prevent the president from gaining a victory on this issue he so cherished or desperately fearful that the appeal of the faith initiative to many minorities might lead them to reevaluate their traditional vote for the Democratic Party.[5] Extremists on the separation of church and state said that no changes were needed because under the current rules, religious groups already could get funded—all they had to do was be sure they were not too religious. Although they claimed that faith-based groups could get funded without any trouble, they also claimed it would be unconstitutional for the law fully to protect the faith character of those faith-based groups.

Jim Towey, head of the White House Office of Faith-Based and Community Initiatives said, "Certainly, the President respects the importance of the constitutional prohibition on funding religion. . . . The wall he wants to tear down is the wall that separates the poor from effective programs."[6]

Other critics tried a different line of attack. They had seen that the charge of unconstitutionality did not convince very many people any longer, so they settled on what they hoped would be a more potent criticism. Because Charitable Choice protects staffing on a religious basis by faith-based groups, these critics claimed the president's initiative must amount to little more than government-funded job discrimination. A popular criticism declared that it was merely a hidden attack on gays or Catholics or Jews. In reality, though, if faith-based groups have a right to staff on a religious basis, then what officials are actually doing in selecting an excellent faith-based group out of all the competitors is simply ensuring that government money is spent effectively and that the needy get the best possible help. The actual rules forbid invidious employment discrimination on grounds such as race, color, national origin, and gender, and no faith-based group is permitted to turn away clients who need help because of their faith or lack of faith.

Critics from the conservative side also hit the Bush plan, worrying that, despite the president's good intentions, it would actually harm Christian ministries. Some feared the changes would lead to federal funding of strange and anti-Christian cults. They seemed to forget that the existing antireligious rules required that government, in theory at least (practice, fortunately, is better), fund only programs with the strange and anti-Christian idea that faith is irrelevant to life and to dealing with problems. They also forgot that, although government isn't competent to judge Christian faithfulness, officials can and do screen out groups that nurture hatred and violate society's rules.

Another criticism was—and is—more serious: Won't collaboration end up strangling faith-based groups in red tape and secularizing restrictions? These critics are on to something: there is a need for caution, even though this criticism overlooks the partnership movement's precise focus on eliminating antireligious rules. Charitable Choice is not perfect, and it only covers a portion of federal funding. In any case, even if all of government's rules were perfect, legal language cannot keep faith-based organizations from losing their faith. Groups that aren't careful can end up dependent on government money (or, for that matter, on money from a corporation or a foundation). In doing so they may well betray their vision and mission just to keep the cash flowing. Chapter 6 discusses challenges like this and points to solutions.

Of course President Bush never proposed that churches, other houses of worship, and faith-based nonprofits should be forced to accept federal funding. He only proposed that religious groups should have an equal opportunity—so they could compete for funding *if they decided it was a good idea for them.* In fact, no group needs to accept federal dollars in order to drift from its mission. All it has to do is to neglect prayer, become careless about the beliefs that guide its employees and shape its programs, and stop cultivating the spiritual life of its staff and governing board.

Government cannot make a faith-based group remain faithful, but it can put a lot of pressure on a group to become faithless, and that is wrong. So what is needed is a movement to require the government to eliminate or modify its rules that ask faith-based groups to trade away their faith in exchange for government money. That's the movement President Bush promised to promote, continuing the reforms that started with the first enactment of Charitable Choice in 1996. No one suggests that faith-based organizations should simply ignore the anti-faith restrictions that often accompany government grants and contracts and take the money anyway. Instead, the faith-based initiative is a movement to make government hospitable to faith-based groups by getting rid of the antireligious bias in government funding programs.

Interview on 9 December 2002 with U. S. Senator Rick Santorum (R-Pennsylvania)

Q: You were a cosponsor in the last Congress with Senator Joe Lieberman (D-Connecticut) of the CARE Act—the Senate's version of faith-based legislation to promote private giving to charities and equal opportunity for faith-based groups to gain federal funding. Although the faith-based initiative is very popular with the public, faith-based legislation ran into a lot of opposition on Capitol Hill the last two years—the CARE Act, for instance, didn't even come to a vote in the Senate. What are some of the reasons for Congress's unwillingness to act?

A: First, the opposition from the left is predictable. Some of these critics do not believe in the basic elements that the faith-based organizations want to spread in the community. These organizations are out there trying to reach people spiritually, and many on the left are uncomfortable with that, and particularly with government involvement with anything that is related to God. I think this view is misguided—it's an opposition based on a flawed understanding of the Constitution or opposition to faith generally.

Another group on the left sees the faith-based debate as an opportunity to further expand their civil rights agenda—which is to remove religious freedom from the Constitution. They are trying to do this by putting economic rights above religious rights, but our nation has always said that religious rights are higher. The opponents are attempting to push faith and religion down in our society, elevating employment rights above the right of people to practice their faith by hiring people with the same religious convictions.

On the right, you have some, like me, who are enthusiastic but also others who are concerned that government, by funding faith-based organizations, will poison them. Certainly there is reason to be concerned. I'm very careful about this. We have to be sure that the government, in giving money, will not erode the very reasons for the success of the faith-based groups—their religious principles and teaching.

The left is against the faith-based initiative for obvious reasons, and the right is split, and there is no real center. People in the middle aren't passionate about this issue either way. They are only passionate about being moderate, being in the center.

The Unlevel Federal Playing Field

So just what would it take to make the federal government more fully honor and not restrict faith-based social service programs? Are federal officials really so dismissive of distinctly religious programs? If things are so bad, how can groups like the Salvation Army get government funds for their programs?

The first task of the original five Centers for Faith-Based and Community Initiatives was to take a close, hard look at their departments' policies and practices to see whether faith-based and community groups seeking funds, information, and technical assistance were welcomed or pushed away. Their detailed audits of programs at HHS, HUD, Justice, Labor, and Education were delivered to the White House Office of Faith-Based and Community Initiatives at the end of July 2001. On 16 August 2001, at a press conference held at the Brookings Institution in Washington, D.C., and broadcast on C-SPAN television, officials from the White House released an overview of the audit reports.

The name of the White House overview was *Unlevel Playing Field: Barriers to Participation by Faith-Based and Community Organizations in Federal Social Service Programs.*[7] The unofficial name is: hanging out the federal government's dirty linen for all to see. Of course, everyone knew there were obstacles (although some insisted on calling all of them constitutionally required limitations). As we have seen, Charitable Choice was a response to actual specific problems discovered by analyzing federal and state laws. *World* magazine, among others, had also exposed unjustifiable restrictions imposed on Christian social ministries. Now the federal government itself was admitting that some good folks with good programs were not treated fairly when they sought federal support.

Unlevel Playing Field details fifteen distinct barriers—obstacles that Christian and other groups might encounter if they approach federal officials. About half of the barriers are rules or practices that create difficulties for all smaller or less-experienced groups—secular or religious—applying for federal help. The other barriers are church-state restrictions that add even more difficulties for faith-based groups.

Of course, not every federal program or agency puts up all of these obstacles. Yet *Unlevel Playing Field* confirmed what has been discovered by just about every group that has thought of applying directly to a federal program for funds: it isn't very easy to find out about federal grants, and if you do, the applications are complicated and rules are piled upon rules. Even experienced groups usually seek professional help to find their way through the federal maze. Even the smallest grants often come with a large burden of regulations. For example, the Department of Justice's Weed and Seed Grant Program references thirteen hundred pages of federal rules—that's a six-inch-tall stack of laws and regulations!

There are other general problems too. Some programs give extra weight to applications from groups that have received federal money in the past, as if their experience doesn't already give them a competitive advantage. Other programs, in a misguided attempt to ensure that services will be coordinated, actually have required that organizations applying for funds demonstrate support from a local government agency—even though that local agency could be competing for exactly the same money!

Sometimes federal officials require applicants to have IRS 501(c)(3) status, even though the law for the program doesn't make such a demand. IRS 501(c)(3) status benefits a group by exempting it from federal taxes and allowing its donors to deduct their contributions (if the donors itemize their deductions on their federal income tax form). It takes time and money to gain 501(c)(3) status, however, and the grant application period may be over and done by the time this is accomplished, or the size of the grant might make the legal and application fees hardly worth the effort. In other words, officials should not insist on this tax status if the law doesn't require it.

In addition to these difficulties, *Unlevel Playing Field* pointed out barriers that specifically afflict faith-based groups seeking federal help. The biggest problem, the report said, was a "pervasive suspicion" by federal officials about the legitimacy of collaboration between faith-based groups and government. The U.S. Constitution's First Amendment protects religious liberty and also forbids the establishment of religion, but officials too often "have focused much more on avoiding the prohibition than on honoring the protection."

To be sure, there are constitutional limits on how government and faith-based organizations can collaborate, but federal rules and practices are often much more restrictive than those limits. In the words of the White House report, officials who run programs that provide federal funds to nongovernmental groups "often seem stuck" in the no-aid separationism framework that the Supreme Court has left behind. Instead of equal treatment, they seem determined to exclude groups that appear to be religious or "too religious."

How widespread is this misplaced fear of trespassing in a forbidden zone if officials include faith-based groups as partners? One incident speaks volumes. The White House wanted a report on what proportion of federal funding went to faith-based organizations. Think about it: you are a grants official, and the Bush White House asks you how much of the money your department gives out went to faith-based service groups. Wouldn't you like to report a large number? It's just like when you were a kid. At the start of the school year, your fourth-grade teacher asked how many books you had read during the summer. Naturally, you totaled up the real books, and then you added the matchbooks, comic books, and anything else you could think of.

The officials' report to the White House showed that HUD's Self-Help Homeownership Opportunity Program in fiscal year 2000 awarded just over half of its $20 million in grants to Habitat for Humanity. What good news it would be to report to the White House that a faith-based organization provided such excellent and innovative services that it won half of the money awarded. Instead of celebrating, however, the officials actually told the White House that no faith-based provider got any of the Self-Help Homeownership money.

Why hide the good news about funding Habitat for Humanity? Here's what *Unlevel Playing Field* says: "With mind-bending logic, HUD officials apparently reasoned that since the government may not aid religion, and yet HUD funds Habitat, then Habitat must not be a faith-based organization." Officials were so afraid that their legitimate funding choice might be judged unconstitutional, they tried to conceal their good deed from the White House!

These worries, which are a holdover from the obsolete no-aid separationism mind-set, lead to many kinds of overly restrictive rules and decisions, as *Unlevel Playing Field* records:

- Some grant reviewers in the Department of Labor assumed that only very secularized groups are eligible for funding.
- Sometimes HUD insisted that groups that look "too religious" (HUD calls them "primarily religious" groups) are barred from receiving federal funds even to support purely secular activities.
- Some local officials believe—in error—that any building that houses a Head Start program must be stripped of all religious symbols and art.
- HHS officials wrongly expanded highly restrictive rules about religion stemming from a court settlement (which has expired, in any case) concerning one abstinence-education

program. They applied those overly restrictive rules to other abstinence-education programs.

- Officials sometimes require religious organizations that apply for funds to agree to abandon their freedom to hire according to faith—not only in programs where Congress has insisted on that requirement but also in programs where there is no such rule.
- Although Congress voted *four times* to put Charitable Choice into federal law, the federal departments that administer the programs for a long time did little or nothing to ensure that the federal funds were spent following the new rules.

Do all these barriers make a significant difference? Can't groups find ways around many or most of them? It turns out to be impossible to figure out just how discouraged faith-based and grassroots groups are when they confront such obstacles. But the fact that not much federal money goes to faith-based groups—despite some striking exceptions—is a sign of the problem.

There is no way to tell precisely how much, or rather how little, such groups get, but there are some indications. It is hard to tell the exact figures for several reasons. Most federal welfare and social services money does not go directly to providers; instead, it goes to state and local governments, and those officials, in turn, award the money to nonprofit and sometimes for-profit groups. These officials, however, rarely tell the federal government how many of those groups are faith-based, and federal officials, who directly award grants, usually don't pay much attention to which recipients are religious, except when they are concerned to screen out the groups that look "too religious."

	Total Grants	Funds Sent to State, Local Governments for Grants, Contracts	Grants Made Directly by Federal Officials
Dept. of Justice	$2.6 billion	$2.0 billion (77%)	$0.6 billion (23%)
Dept. of Labor	$6.8 billion	$6.0 billion (88%)	$0.8 billion (12%)
HUD	$28.0 billion	$25.6 billion (91%)	$2.4 billion (9%)
Dept. of Education	$29.0 billion	$23.9 billion (82%)	$5.1 billion (18%)
HHS	$185.1 billion	$160.2 billion (87%)	$24.9 billion (13%)

Source: These figures are from *Unlevel Playing Field* and date from fiscal year 2000 or 2001.

Unlevel Playing Field does give a few solid numbers, and they tell a sad tale. If you look around in your community, you can see that churches, other houses of worship, and faith-based parachurch programs are a significant, and often large, part of the network of service groups that provide emergency housing, run food pantries, provide job training, help prevent drug addiction, fight juvenile gangs, promote sexual abstinence, spark community economic development, and much more. Yet when it comes to federal funding of such services:

- The Office of Justice Programs of the Department of Justice projected that in fiscal year 2001 only 0.3 percent—that's just one-third of one percent—of the funds it would distribute to state and local governments would be won by faith-based providers.
- The Department of Education calculated that in fiscal year 2000, faith-based or secular community-based groups won only 25 of the 1,091 grants it awarded, which is just 2 percent of the grants.
- In the same year, faith-based organizations won about 16 percent of the funds distributed through HUD's Continuum of Care process for services to the homeless.
- When the Department of Labor studied how its Workforce Investment Act funds had been expended in five cities, it discovered that the local workforce boards in all five cities contracted with religious providers, but the proportions were minimal: 1 percent in three cities, 6 percent in one city, and a high of only 10 percent in the fifth city.
- In Wisconsin in 2000, faith-based groups won federal and state welfare funds covered by Charitable Choice in the various administrative regions from a low of 1 percent to a high of 16 percent.

Thankfully, these paltry figures did not tell the whole story—remember the HUD program that works so extensively with Habitat for Humanity, and think about the long history of government support for Salvation Army, Catholic Charities, Jewish Community Services, and Lutheran Services of America. At the end of this chapter we will see that, more recently, the pattern of funding has changed dramatically in some places. Of course there is no *right* percentage of government funding for faith-based providers. If faith-based groups are the best providers of some service, they should get the funds. If in another program the best providers are secular, then few or no faith groups should be getting any of those funds.

Still, these numbers, the HUD officials' bashfulness about telling their good news, and all those restrictive practices that afflict faith-based applicants and all smaller and newer applicants, make it all too clear that the federal government has been far from encouraging and enlisting "neighborhood healers."

Leveling the Federal Playing Field

Bitter opposition sprang up when President Bush announced his faith-based initiative. Angry resistance also greeted the proposed Community Solutions Act, by which Charitable Choice could be expanded to new programs. As it turns out, however, the opponents did not get the last word. Regardless of what many in Congress think now, under the Clinton administration large majorities of senators and representatives voted to put Charitable Choice into several federal laws. The Supreme Court's decisions have also continued on the equal treatment track and not the "no-aid" direction so that today the trend is faith-friendly, not anti-faith.

At this point, much of what needs to be done to level the federal playing field is a matter of reforming the way grants are administrated, rather than passing new laws or even revising regulations. Still, some regulatory or legislative change is needed to get rid of barriers. Congress has written into some federal funding programs the requirement that all grantees, including faith-based organizations, must agree to ignore faith in their employment decisions. For programs like that to become fully faith-friendly, Congress will have to change its mind. Similarly, some of HUD's extreme restrictions on faith-based organizations are written into program regulations, and changing regulations is a long and difficult process that gives defenders of the status quo many chances to slow down or stop reform.

More often, though, the overly broad restrictions on faith and the overly complicated procedures and snarls of red tape are the result of past administrative decisions, and they can be changed by new administrative decisions. That's not to say that change is easy. Getting the federal government to actually change how it operates is at least as difficult as getting a supertanker to turn around. But reforms that stay within the boundaries of laws, regulations, and court decisions are changes the president can make without waiting for Congress to act.

In fact, making administrative changes so that the federal government operates more effectively is a specific responsibility of the president and of the secretaries of the various federal departments. Every president and administration works at such administrative reform. President Ronald Reagan, for instance, worked hard to eliminate waste in federal programs. During the last administration, Vice President Al Gore was in charge of a sweeping "reinventing government" initiative, which emphasized performance over paperwork.

For President George W. Bush, expanding the role of faith-based and community-based groups in federally funded programs is not just a legislative goal, a theme for speeches, or a way to fire up supporters. It is a key administrative reform. Creating a level playing field for religious organizations and for smaller charities is part of the Bush administration's own government-reform initiative. That's why the president created not only a special White House office to promote the cause but also special Centers within the major federal social-program departments.

Bush was not interested in simply yelling from the White House at federal officials who administer grant programs. Instead, he sought an inner process of administrative reform inside the departments. In his view, promoting collaboration with faith-based and grassroots groups should be the departments' own initiatives. That's why the *President's Management Agenda*—his administrative reform blueprint—includes the faith-based and community initiative as an integral part of the president's "strategy for improving the management and performance of the federal government."[8] It is also why, in December 2002, the president issued an executive order calling for equal treatment principles to be applied in all social service programs that use federal funds, whether those programs are overseen by federal, state, or local officials.

So what are federal officials doing to level the playing field and extend a welcome to faith-based service organizations? Even before

Unlevel Playing Field was unveiled, the Administration on Aging at HHS had agreed to drop its anticompetition requirement, so that groups seeking funding from the National Family Caregiver Support Program no longer had to show support from their local area Agency on Aging—which could be a competitor for the same federal grant. Of course, most of the needed changes will take a lot longer to achieve than that quick response!

One important change is a determined and more accessible new federal outreach to faith-based and grassroots organizations. Usually federal grants are announced in the dry text of the *Federal Register*. In addition, federal departments and their various welfare and social service programs have websites and, often, toll-free numbers to inform the public about available grants, to describe how to apply for funds, and to provide technical assistance—specialized help for completing a grant application and for operating the social services. Few people, however, other than professional grant writers, daily scan the *Federal Register* or departmental websites. Of course church-related groups that have had good reasons to believe federal officials are not interested in them have had even less reason to bother checking these information sources.

So now federal officials themselves are reaching out, even more widely and more energetically than under the previous administration. For example, the Center for Faith-Based and Community Initiatives at the Department of Education started in 2001 to offer workshops on the president's initiative and on grant writing that drew thousands of clergy and grassroots leaders.

Starting in the fall of 2002, the White House Office of Faith-Based and Community Initiatives and the Centers in the departments began jointly offering day-long conferences on President Bush's initiative and on seeking federal grants. The first one, in Atlanta, drew an overflow crowd of more than fifteen hundred faith and community leaders. Of course, White House and Center officials have been offering workshops and speeches at gatherings put on by others. These have included the Christian Community Development Association's annual conference, the Faith Roundtable session at the legislative conference of the National Black Caucus of State Legislators, the annual convention of the Islamic Society of North America, the gathering of United Methodist attorneys and clergy who direct social programs, the public affairs and religious liberty directors of the Seventh-Day Adventist Church, and national, regional, and local Jewish associations.

The website of the Office of Faith-Based and Community Initiatives features President Bush's speeches spotlighting the role of faith-based services and makes it easy to print a copy of his blueprint for reform, "Rallying the Armies of Compassion." It is also the place to go to download a booklet on "Guidance to Faith-Based and Community Organizations on Partnering with the Federal Government" and the *Unlevel Playing Field* report. The site also has links to the Centers for Faith-Based and Community Initiatives, which can also be accessed through their respective departments' websites.

Today, federal grant announcements often explicitly state that religious organizations are eligible to apply (unless the grants can only be awarded to secular entities like states or businesses). For example, HUD's March 2002 SuperNOFA announcement—the combined announcement of $2.2 billion in grants available directly from HUD through more than forty programs—emphasizes that faith-based and other community-based groups are equally eligible with other nonprofit organizations in many of the programs. The announcement for fiscal year 2002 grants from the Juvenile Mentoring Program of the Department of Justice specifically notes, "faith-based organizations are also encouraged to apply." In August 2002 the Department of Education published draft rules for state education officials on how they are to administer grants to provide special academic services to students in poorly performing schools. These grants are part of the Bush education reform law—the "No Child Left Behind Act." The rules to guide the state officials detail the eligibility of faith-based organizations—including religious schools—for the federal funds.

HUD goes beyond verbal encouragement. Pointing out that "civic organizations, congregations, and faith-based and other community-based organizations" have not been fruitfully utilized in the past, the 2002 SuperNOFA announced that inclusion of such groups in HUD-funded services was one of Secretary Mel Martinez's seven policy priorities. So, just as grant applicants who can prove that their HUD-funded program will make a measurable difference will receive bonus points when their applications are rated, applicants who are faith-based or community-based or who partner with faith-based or grassroots groups also receive extra points. The Department of Education, completing an initiative started under the Clinton administration, has modified the rules for some grant programs so that "novice applicants"—organizations that have never before received a federal grant—have a better chance of winning funding.

Federal officials are also changing or clarifying the restrictions and freedoms that apply to faith-based groups that accept government money. For example, the draft guidance for the "No Child Left Behind Act" states that faith-based groups may not use the federal funds to pay for purely religious activities such as worship or religious instruction. It also affirms that they may offer such activities on a voluntary basis, separately from the federally funded academic services, and that they cannot be required by state education officials to "give up their religious character or identification." Another example is that the overly restrictive rules about faith that HHS officials had been misapplying to abstinence-education funding have been rewritten.

In December 2002 President Bush directed FEMA, the Federal Emergency Management Agency, to stop its biased practice of refusing to give financial assistance to help the recovery of faith-based nonprofits that are devastated along with other organizations when natural disasters such as hurricanes and earthquakes strike. By executive order, the president also modified long-standing rules for federal contracting so that religious organizations can now contract to provide goods or services to the federal government without giving up their liberty to staff on a religious basis. That same month, HUD announced the elimination of some regulations and the modification of others to end unjustifiable restrictions on faith-based groups that accept HUD money and unjustifiable rules that excluded other faith-based groups from being able to partner with federal programs.

Both HHS and the Department of Labor have allocated millions of dollars for special programs to help inexperienced and smaller religious and secular groups partner with government. The Labor grants were awarded in the summer of 2002 to promote partnerships between One-Stop Career Centers, which deliver federally funded employment training services, and community and faith groups that also provide job-preparation services. Twelve states received funds to develop innovative ways to connect the faith-based and grassroots programs with the centers, and nine intermediary organizations were funded to expand their services that assist sacred and secular groups.

In October 2002, HHS awarded nearly $25 million to twenty-one groups as part of a new Compassion Capital Fund, authorized by Congress at the request of President Bush. The winners are intermediaries that are trusted by grassroots and faith-based groups, and the federal funds will enable them to expand their services to train the small groups to improve their programs, become better able to obtain grants and other income, develop performance measures, and better their record keeping and management abilities. To give another example, the Substance Abuse and Mental Health Services Administration, a subdivision of HHS, has started contracting with faith-sensitive technical assistance providers such as We Care America.

Pat Robertson, former presidential candidate and founder of the Christian Broadcasting Network, the 700 Club, and Regent University, was very skeptical about the idea of expanded partnerships between the federal government and faith-based services. Reporters were quick to pounce when Operation Blessing, the Robertson program that provides assistance to needy people in the United States and around the world, won federal funds in the fall of 2002 to provide training and small grants to affiliated social programs. Robertson released a statement on 29 October 2002, which included the following:

My initial concern about the faith-based initiative, as it was originally presented, was the potentially intrusive nature of government into the outreach programs of faith-based organizations. I also was concerned that small faith-based organizations might lose their independence by becoming totally dependent on government grants.

I am delighted that the faith-based initiative, as currently presented, does not have the same intrusive quality as was first laid out in initial proposals.

Secondly, I want to say that Operation Blessing, which has an annual income of cash and gifts-in-kind approaching $50 million, will continue to partner with nongovernmental sources to provide humanitarian relief across America and around the world. The $500,000 grant from the Compassion Capital Fund will allow Operation Blessing to provide additional training and assistance to a network of more than 120 smaller relief groups across the United States. Operation Blessing will continue to equip and train the smaller, faith-based organizations to develop more effective programs in their own local communities. This will result in more food and relief supplies being delivered to the people who need it most.

Among other noteworthy innovations, both the Department of Labor and HHS have undertaken special initiatives to educate state and local officials about spending the federal funds they receive in a faith- and community-friendly way. Early in 2002, Labor published information packets for faith-based organizations (with a cover featuring a burning bush) and for community-based organizations, suggesting how such groups can help their own members obtain needed job-training services and how the groups can partner with One-Stop Career Centers. At the same time, Labor produced folders with sample slide-show presentations for state and local workforce training officials to use in reaching out to faith-based and community-based organizations.

The subdivisions of HHS that administer federal funds covered by Charitable Choice (welfare, community services, and drug treatment) have been organizing workshops to guide state and local officials. Also, at the end of 2002 official guidelines were proposed on what state and local officials have to do to comply with the Charitable Choice rules.

States and Charitable Choice

Many state and local leaders have not waited for the Bush administration to remind them of their obligation to adhere to the Charitable Choice rules. Officials in many places across the nation have pioneered outreach strategies, and they have reformed funding programs, making them more hospitable to churches, parachurch programs, and smaller charities. They had started to "rally the armies of compassion" before the White House even started using that phrase. Remember, these innovations by state and local governments are particularly important because these governments, in addition to spending a great deal of their own money, are the actual administrators of the bulk of federal welfare and social spending.

Only a sketchy overview of changes is possible, of course, because the fifty states (and the District of Columbia and the U.S. territories) are so diverse. Some have pioneered collaboration reforms, and some are still resisting change. (For more detail and to keep up with the changes, check the websites of the Center for Public Justice, the Hudson Institute's Faith in Communities Initiative, and the Welfare Information Network. Contact information is given in the resource section at the end of the book.) Following are some of the significant reforms:

In several states, the governor (Texas), lieutenant governor (Virginia), legislature (Georgia, Wisconsin), or welfare department (Ohio) has initiated a task force or hearings to determine the barriers that hamper faith and community groups and to recommend ways to remove those obstacles. In these and other states and localities, such task forces, commissions, other research, Congress's passage of Charitable Choice, or just the desire for services that are more effective have led to changes both small and large. Some of the changes remove church-state barriers. Other changes make it easier for all groups to partner with government programs.

Reforms to make government less forbidding to smaller and less experienced groups include the development of staff positions or offices designated as liaisons to faith-based and community-based groups (check the Center for Public Justice website for a list of liaisons). These liaisons are like a greeter at the door, providing an entry point for organizations that otherwise might find the government bureaucracy baffling, with no obvious phone number to call for information or help and no one able to give a clear explanation of the dos and don'ts for faith-based participants. As well as reaching out to nontraditional partners, the liaisons also often "reach in," explaining to other officials why groups that value their faith character often find government rules too suffocating. They explain what the officials should do in response to new guidelines like Charitable Choice.

In Virginia, state welfare officials asked a coordinator of volunteers to become the liaison to faith and community groups. In Texas, each of the eleven Department of Human Services regional offices and each of the twenty-eight local workforce investment boards (which are in charge of the One-Stop Career Centers) have a designated liaison.

Oklahoma has a special Office of Faith-Based and Community Initiatives.

In Indiana, when Democrat Frank O'Bannon took over as governor, he directed welfare officials to promote partnerships. The result is FaithWorks Indiana, a special program, complete with a toll-free number and website, that has organized conferences for interested novice organizations, provides training in grant writing and individualized assistance, and offers easy access to information about new government funding opportunities.

Some cities also have thriving liaisons. Indianapolis pioneered the idea under former mayor Steve Goldsmith with the "Front Porch Alliance." (Goldsmith is now chairman of the board of directors of the Corporation for National and Community Service under President George W. Bush.) This was an innovative office through which city hall officials connected community groups, including churches, with city programs and helped the groups cut red tape and access government and private funds. Philadelphia and Memphis, among other places, also have energetic faith and community liaisons who work to empower faith and community groups.

Some state or local agencies have redesigned their grant and contract procedures to make them less intimidating to newcomers and smaller groups. Texas, for instance, has offered "Innovation Grants," which are relatively small awards for services proposed not by government officials but by the applicants themselves. The announcements outlined specific needs and then asked charities and churches to propose how they would overcome the problems.

Pennsylvania's welfare department redesigned grant application forms to require less writing and time from applicants.

Looking for an effective way to inform women about their risk of suffering heart disease and about lifestyle changes that decrease the risk, the human services department of Mercer County, New Jersey (Trenton area), decided to partner with community organizations, including religious ones. To encourage participation by small and inexperienced groups, the grants were made small, the request for proposals was short—just one page to describe the grants and one page on the problem to be addressed—and the information requested from applicants was brief.

What about the overly restrictive rules that have repelled many faith-based groups that otherwise might consider collaborating with state-run programs? Are states leveling the playing field? The big liberator here is Charitable Choice. Remember that it is a federal rule, but it applies to federal funds that in most cases go directly to state or local authorities, which in turn give out the money to nongovernmental groups to provide welfare, community, and drug treatment services.

So are states and local agencies (counties and regional welfare coalitions, Community Action Agencies) changing their practices when they spend the federal money on grants and contracts? Are they complying with Charitable Choice? It is hard to reform government practices, so it would not be a surprise if the new rules for SAMHSA drug treatment funding, adopted at the end of 2000, have not made much difference yet. Charitable Choice was applied to the core funding for Community Action Agencies in 1998 and to funding for welfare services as long ago as 1996. Officials administering funding for welfare services, if not the community services money, have had many years to make changes. As it turns out, change has been slow and uneven—but it is spreading and accelerating, as we will see.

Still, when the Center for Public Justice surveyed state officials in the spring and summer of 2000 to grade them on their compliance, the report card was shameful. Of the fifty-four states and territories, just twelve, only 22 percent, earned a passing grade (see the Center for Public Justice website for the grades). Forty earned Fs for violating one or more of the new requirements (two states refused to say what they were doing). The states with passing grades in 2000 were Arizona, Arkansas, California, Illinois, Indiana, Michigan, North Carolina, Ohio, Pennsylvania, Texas, Virginia, and Wisconsin.

It was not true, however, that all the states that failed were dead set against working with congregations and faith-based nonprofit groups. In fact, that was not the case at all. Many over the past few years had become very friendly to such organizations, reaching out to include them in referral networks or to draw on their volunteers as mentors for welfare families. Sometimes the states even welcomed new faith-based groups to apply for funding for their services. Despite the welcome, however, the overly restrictive rules still remained on paper. The new partnerships required the officials and the faith leaders to adopt a "don't ask and don't tell" attitude to the restrictions. Practice was flexible, but the rules were still very restrictive—clearly not a very solid foundation for working together.

However, besides the states that got passing grades in 2000, others have improved their compliance since the survey. Some states have responded positively to create a new framework of rules to govern their search for effective social service providers.

For example, some governors have issued executive orders directing all state agencies that receive federal funds covered by Charitable Choice to make sure they comply with all of the new requirements (Texas, Colorado, Arkansas, and Oklahoma). A few states have even decided to apply those federal Charitable Choice rules beyond the federal funds also to certain state or local funds (Wisconsin, Arizona, Texas).

What had to be changed in these states in order to reform their rules? Sometimes laws or regulations had to be clarified so officials could no longer exclude organizations they judged to be "very religious" or "too religious" (or in technical terms, "pervasively sectarian"). Some states have modified their rules for contracting so that, when federal funds covered by Charitable Choice are involved, it is clear that faith-based organizations retain their liberty to staff on a religious basis (for example, Texas changed its procurement law in 1998 and Virginia in 2001). Some states, such as Texas and Indiana, write into their contracts with faith-based organizations a paragraph specifying the religious liberty rights that Charitable Choice guarantees to the people who are looking for help.

In a number of states, either counties or regional agencies have the major responsibility to design the welfare services. In some of these places, the state welfare authorities have given explicit guidance that Charitable Choice must guide how those lower-level officials spend their welfare money to buy services for the poor. New York sent a guidance letter in May 2002. Arkansas amended their guidance booklet for regional welfare authorities in 2000, and Ohio sent official guidance to counties in 1998. The state welfare department in California was required by the legislature to start developing Charitable Choice regulations for counties by July 2000—although regulations had not been issued more than two years later.

A few states have been reluctant to go along with Charitable Choice on the grounds that their own state constitutions require a greater separation between church and state than does the U.S. Constitution. (About two-thirds of state constitutions include restrictive so-called "Blaine amendments"—the fruit of an anti-Catholic movement in the last few decades of the nineteenth century—but state and federal courts dispute just how restrictive these church-state provisions really are.) Charitable Choice, in fact, requires that states whose constitutions restrict giving state funds to religious organizations keep their federal welfare dollars separate and comply with Charitable Choice when spending the federal funds.

One of the states with very restrictive language is Georgia, but in 2002 Georgia's Democratic governor and the legislature agreed on a new state law that works around that restriction so the state can comply with Charitable Choice and build new partnerships. The law directs welfare officials to keep federal and state welfare money separate and to comply with Charitable Choice when using the federal money to buy services. It also assures state officials that it is not illegal for them to spend a bit of state money to administer the federal funds according to the federal rules.

EXPLOSIVE GROWTH IN GOVERNMENT PARTNERSHIPS WITH FAITH-BASED GROUPS

There have been many changes: the action Congress took in adopting Charitable Choice several times, states that have modified their actual rules, places that have become more flexible in practice even if the rules on the books still remain restrictive, new outreach initiatives, revised grant programs, and more. What difference have these changes made?

Unlevel Playing Field showed that officials spending federal money often look to every service group except faith-based ones when they seek partners. Times and practices change, however, and there is no uniform picture across the nation or among the various levels of government. Still, if you want an overview these days of how states are responding to Charitable Choice, you would have to say that Congress's leadership in passing the charter of religious liberty for faith-based providers is starting to pay off. The result has been dramatic changes in the partners chosen by states to help them deliver welfare and social services.

The evidence is in the hard numbers. In early 2000, Amy Sherman published a report on how extensively officials in nine states were contracting with faith-based organizations for welfare services. In early 2002, she reported again on how officials in those states were doing, this time asking not only about how they used their federal welfare funds but also their federal Community Services Block Grant money and their federal drug-treatment money. Here is what she discovered.[9]

State	Number of Contracts, 2000 Study	Number of Contracts, 2002 Study	$ Total, 2000	$ Total, 2002
California	11	107	$1,887,608	$15,655,024
Illinois	7	69	$1,819,500	$6,209,743
Massachusetts	3	22	$320,000	$6,809,692
Michigan	9	129	$744,470	$21,858,717
Mississippi	0	0	$0	$0
New York	7	32	$1,860,705	$9,060,873
Texas	4	19	$130,449	$18,276,912
Virginia	3	6	$114,568	$2,381,711
Wisconsin	10	101	$686,167	$8,236,560
Totals	54	485	$7,563,467	$88,489,232

What an encouraging story the numbers tell! Outside of Mississippi, which persisted in its determination to ignore the opportunity to collaborate with faith-based organizations, each of these states—selected because of their geographical diversity, urban population centers, and different attitudes about collaboration—made enormous strides between 2000 and 2002 in welcoming faith-based organizations as partners in providing welfare and social services. Taking the states together, the number of contracts increased by nine times, and the total value of the contracts increased more than tenfold.

Here is undeniable evidence that Charitable Choice is making a real difference for faith-based organizations and for the people who depend on government-funded services. Discriminatory practices that excluded good service providers from being government's partners simply because those providers were religious or "too religious" are being changed. The faith-based initiative is not just talk. It is not just a matter of hoped-for changes. Federal, state, and local officials have not simply been paying lip service to the growing consensus that faith-based services must be brought back into the center of the nation's social assistance effort. State and local policies and practices are being transformed, not uniformly, but in many places substantially. In short, the playing field is being leveled.

WE WOULD WORK WITH GOVERNMENT AGAIN

But wait. Do those numbers simply mean that government is seducing those groups into trading their faith for dollars? Maybe the expanded contracting is just more of the same old thing: officials willing to work with faith-based organizations but only when those organizations are willing to mask or sideline their religion. Sure, some faith-based groups have found ways to remain faithful in that old framework, but isn't it still a bad framework and a bad bargain? After all, it hasn't been that long since most states got Fs on compliance with Charitable Choice.

It is true and important to emphasize: state compliance with Charitable Choice is spotty. Often, even where there are many more contracts, the rules the government insists on are still too restrictive. Even if officials are willing to wink at the rules and to actually permit more freedom in practice, such mere toleration of faithful practices is not the solid foundation for a true partnership that is required by Charitable Choice and the Supreme Court's equal treatment doctrine. Yet, as we saw, government rules are being changed in many places. And now we have fresh evidence that many faith-based organizations that are accepting government money to provide services are finding a hospitable environment instead of confronting all the old restrictions.

Inside the Beltway—that is, in Washington, D.C., and its suburbs, where Congress, the key federal government offices, national think tanks, and top civil rights and church-state separationist organizations find their homes—Charitable Choice is often merely a topic for shouting matches, a supposedly extremist idea. Yet there is a huge disconnect between what goes on inside the Beltway and what happens outside it, in the states and communities.

Inside the Beltway	In Real Life
Charitable Choice is often treated as an oddball Bush idea that Congress might, or likely will not, adopt.	Charitable Choice was enacted into law four times during the Clinton administration.
Charitable Choice is often talked about as a hypothetical set of requirements that can be favored or dismissed, depending on one's taste.	Because Congress actually has applied the new rules to several federal social-spending programs that send money to state and local governments, state and community governments are changing their actual contracting rules and practices.
Charitable Choice is treated as a matter of speculative fears and hopes.	Because Charitable Choice has been a federal requirement in several programs for a significant period of time, we can see its actual consequences. Those real-world consequences do not match the fears of the liberals who expect rampant religious coercion or the fears of conservatives who expect rampant secularization.

The faith initiative—the Revolution of Compassion—is making a real difference for faith-based groups that want to be respected partners. You can hear stories of fruitful collaborations at the annual conventions of the Christian Community Development Association, where the leaders and supporters of hundreds of evangelical church-based community service groups gather to worship together, to celebrate, and to learn how to serve more effectively. Or talk to Salvation Army folks who are grateful that a new government attitude and new rules are making it easier to offer holistic services that acknowledge that hurting people have hearts and souls as well as bodies, brains, and feelings.

Or listen to Kurt M. Senske, president of Lutheran Social Services of the South, headquartered in San Antonio, Texas. LSS, like other affiliates of Lutheran Services of America, has long collaborated with government as a religiously affiliated provider of services. Yet Senske believes that the new rules are important even for groups like his that have a long history of receiving government funding. That's because in a well-intentioned effort to ensure that clients of faith-based programs not be pressured about religion, overly restrictive regulations—he calls them "thou shalt nots"—were adopted. Those rules pressured groups to downplay and hide their religious character.

Now, however, the "thou shalt nots" are being removed. The faith-based initiative has brought in a different government attitude, Senske writes, a "culture of acceptance that faith-based organizations

[can] provide services to those in need and often do an even better job than their secular counterparts," because they "provide a value-added dimension of care through their voluntary offering of spiritual care in addition to the other care provided." The new attitude, he says, means "We do not have to downplay the fact that we are Lutheran or even Christian. We are not barred from offering voluntary programs to address the spiritual needs of the nearly 26,000 children, elderly and poor whom we serve annually throughout Texas and Louisiana."[10]

We also have the witness of hundreds of faith-based groups that are contracting with state and local governments using federal funds covered by Charitable Choice. Amy Sherman's recent look at contracting by faith-based organizations, reported above, examined not only the original nine states surveyed but also six additional states (Arkansas, Colorado, Florida, Indiana, Ohio, and Oklahoma). At the start of 2002, these fifteen states together contracted with a total of 587 congregations and parachurch ministries (for a total of $123,784,621 in contracts).

In spring 2002 Amy Sherman and colleague John Green, with the assistance of a survey center, asked the leaders of all 587 groups a set of questions about their experiences working with government. Two-thirds of the leaders responded, so Amy and John can report on the experiences of 389 faith-based organizations that contract with state and local governments using funds covered by Charitable Choice.[11]

What are those experiences? The survey reports:

Charitable Choice requires	What is the practice?
A level playing field. No group is to be excluded from funding because it is religious or "too religious" (or because it is secular)	In these fifteen states, all kinds of faith-based groups are winning contracts—groups religious only in name or motivation and also groups that embody their faith in the organization's practices and in the way services are designed and delivered; not only faith-based nonprofits but also congregations; not only large congregations but also small ones. More than half of the faith-based groups only started collaborating with government after the rules were changed following the first enactment of Charitable Choice in 1996.
A change in the rules that pressure faith-based organizations to hide or set aside important aspects of their religious character	Many of the contractors are the kinds of faith-based organizations that in the past were routinely judged to be "too religious" to be eligible to collaborate with government. The survey calls just over a quarter of the contractors "fully expressive" groups—their activities and appearance are obviously religious. About half of the contractors were either religiously distinctive organizations or engaged in religiously distinctive practices. Only about a quarter of the contractors were "non-expressive"—the kinds of groups that used to be called "religiously affiliated" organizations.

In addition, of these faith-based organizations that have decided to accept government money:

- More than two-thirds said it was "very important" that they could control who was on their board of directors (for example, by selecting clergy).
- About half said it was "very important" that they were free to maintain a religious environment where they deliver services (for example, by hanging religious artwork).
- Two-thirds said it was "very important" or "somewhat important" that they retained their freedom to hire on a religious basis.

In short, these faith-based organizations have gone after government funds, but that does not mean they are wishy-washy about their faith basis.

Charitable Choice requires	What is the practice?
Strong protections for the religious liberty of clients	Large majorities of the faith-based contractors tell clients they are not required to take part in inherently religious activities like Bible reading and prayer if they do not wish to. Furthermore, they can choose a different provider if they object to being served by a faith-based group.
Faith-based contractors must not divert government money away from welfare or social services to inherently religious activities	More than two-thirds of these faith-based contractors keep government funds in a separate account from their private funds so they can easily keep track of what money is spent for what kind of activity. The groups that are most careful about the requirement are the ones for which it makes a real difference because of their commitment to being very religious as an organization—congregations and "fully expressive" nonprofits. Such contractors do not leave these matters to chance, either, but have adopted specific strategies to make sure the guidelines are respected.

Do these responses tell us enough? Maybe Charitable Choice's requirements are met, and everything looks fine on paper. Yet isn't it true that when an ant climbs into bed with an elephant, the ant never gets a good night's sleep? Charitable Choice sounds good, but what about red tape, getting hooked on government money, and all those other problems?

The survey did quiz a lot of faith-based providers, but it still was a limited sample. Groups in other states might have a differ-

ent experience, or the same groups might think differently about
their contracting experience further down the road after they have
collaborated for more years. Those are real possibilities, but here
is what these 389 faith-based contractors said about their experiences so far:

- 92 percent said they experienced only "some" or "very little"
  intrusion into their affairs by officials monitoring the contracts.
- 92 percent said they only had "some" or "very little" difficulty
  applying for the funds.
- 71 percent said the reporting requirements imposed only
  "some" or "very little" burden on them.
- 89 percent said they "disagree" or "strongly disagree" that
  accepting government funds threatened the faith character
  of their organization.
- 89 percent said they "disagree" or "strongly disagree" that
  taking government money made it harder to criticize government policy based on their faith convictions.
- 90 percent said they "disagree" or "strongly disagree" that
  accepting government money was likely to reduce the amount
  of private donations given to them.

So, given what they had experienced in partnering with government in this new era in which officials realize they need to replace
hostility with hospitality, would these churches and parachurch
organizations do it all over again? Fully 92 percent said, "Yes,"
they were likely to seek a similar contract from government in the
future.

Is Charitable Choice making a difference? Is the faith-based initiative changing practice so that it is not just a matter of fine words
from President Bush and other officials? What can we do but echo
the faith-based contractors in the survey and answer, "Yes."

4

In Partnership with Business

Faith-based organizations provide the building blocks your community needs, including social, spiritual and developmental services.

Bank of America

When Christian ministries think about possible connections with businesses, the first thing, and sometimes the only thing, they think about is the possibility of winning financial support. They hope that businessmen and women, Christian or not, who see their ministries' good works of service will make a donation. It is true that many businesses, as part of their contribution to the community, do generously give money to faith-based as well as secular organizations, but money is not the only way companies and religious charities can be connected. Businesspeople have insight and expertise to share, and businesses and faith-based groups are forming partnerships to help welfare recipients and other hard-to-employ men and women become self-sustaining.

In this chapter we will look at some of the ways church-based social programs and businesses can work together in service of

Jesus and a Job

A "Convoy of Hope" can best be described as a combination carnival and shopping mall of social services, intended to reach out to needy children and their families. Parents and their kids enjoy games, rides, balloons, and clowns; they also receive practical help at "ministry booths" designated for counseling, health screening, job placement, food distribution, and even haircuts. On 23 October 1999, over one thousand volunteers representing local churches, organizations, agencies, and hospitals gathered at Patterson Park in Baltimore, Maryland, for a Convoy of Hope outreach.

Literally hundreds of families arrived early and patiently stood in line waiting for the gates to open. I (Dave) decided to walk along the line, meet the guests, and ask them why they came and what they expected. As I mingled with the crowd I came across a man in his early thirties named Jim, who was accompanied by his eight-year-old son.

"Why did you come today?" I asked him.

Jim responded edgily, "I need a job, but nobody will hire me because of my problems." Then looking down at his son in embarrassment, he said, "I don't want my son to think his dad is a bum. I want him to be proud of me." Jim went on to explain that he had a hard time getting work because he had a long history of changing jobs.

Later that day I talked to others as they left the Convoy of Hope event. I approached a single mother named Charlotte and asked, "Are you glad you came?" A warm smile lit up her face. "I have been having a hard time," she replied, "but today is a good day."

Then Charlotte's lips began to quiver, her voice broke, and tears rolled down her cheeks. "Yes, today is a good day," she continued. "A pastor invited me to his church. I had to tell him that I don't have anything to wear, but he said, 'Jesus doesn't see the outside, just the inside.'" By now her tears had turned to sobs. I hugged her and told her, "Jesus loves you, and so do we." After a little more conversation, I asked, "Do you have a job?"

"I'm embarrassed to go for a job interview because of my clothes," Charlotte confided. "Besides, I don't have a car or anyone to take care of my children."

As I thought later about Jim and Charlotte, I could hear in my mind a typical response to situations like theirs: "People like that should just pull themselves together, get a job, and support themselves!" In reality, that's exactly what Jim and Charlotte wanted to do. They had the desire, but they lacked something else. Clearly, if they were going to support themselves, they were going to need help from others.

What Charlotte and Jim needed was a bridge—a pathway to employment made up of supportive people and services along the way, with a welcoming employer at the other end. For faith-based organizations to help Jim and Charlotte to succeed, they need to be in partnership with business.

the needy. We will provide some examples of positive cooperation, discuss major barriers to collaboration, and consider ways to overcome those problems. We will also consider keys to building fruitful partnerships.

Who Helps the Needy?

It may be surprising, but one of the major barriers that stands in the way of expansive and fruitful collaboration between businesses and faith-based organizations has been thrown up by faith leaders. As we have talked with businessmen and women, we have often heard this kind of comment: "Faith-based groups often have a welfare mentality that begins with the premise that we, corporate leaders, do not have vision and compassion." Or, "I can't tell you how many times ministry leaders have come to me with the attitude, 'Okay, just give us money so we can do the *important* work.'"

Such comments suggest that church and parachurch leaders may not really believe that businesspeople care much about the communities in which they live and work, about the nation's health, or about the poor. What a hasty and mistaken generalization that is! Of course in business, just as in all walks of life, some people are out for their own good and care little about others. Yet many businessmen and women get great satisfaction from being able to build sustainable companies that offer gainful employment as well as useful goods and services. They know that jobs and tax revenue are major contributions to the welfare of both families and communities. As well, these businesses give money and talent to faith-based and secular community-serving groups.

A much-needed first step in building fruitful collaborations with businesses is for faith leaders to engage in "kingdom diplomacy." By this we mean conveying to business leaders, "We need your friendship, expertise, and resources to fulfill the calling we both have to serve our neighbors."

One good example of such kingdom diplomacy is the Halftime organization. Bob Buford founded Halftime to bridge the divide between ministries and businesses by "identifying leaders who are seeking to serve God, helping them discover their gifting and passions, and providing them with avenues of opportunities to serve." Halftime creates "Collision points" where business professionals are matched with Christian ministries, churches, and non-profit organizations. Faith-based groups benefit by learning how to apply market-based principles and the business professionals find fulfillment in lending their skills to serve those in need.[1]

FINANCIAL SUPPORT FROM BUSINESSES

Besides the good works that companies themselves do as they create jobs and provide services and products, many businesses contribute to the greater good by financially supporting community-serving organizations. Over the past few decades numerous corporations have created foundations as their channel for making donations to community groups. Establishing foundations promotes fiscal accountability, overcomes some legal difficulties, and promotes so-called "cause marketing," by which the corporation's name is associated with good works as a marketing tool.

Yet, as Bob Buford, who works with corporate leaders nationwide, points out, "Giving USA"—the major study on giving—indicates that 80 percent of philanthropy in the United States is individual, with the other 20 percent from corporations and foundations. Because that individual giving is spread out, it doesn't get sufficient study. "In individual philanthropy," Buford explains, "about half goes to faith-based groups, but when you look at corporate philanthropy, the amount to the religious community is negligible."[2]

Let's look at three distinct ways businesses relate to faith-based service organizations.

1. Some Support Faith-Based as Well as Secular Groups

A study by the Capital Research Center reveals that in 1998 the ten largest American corporations gave less than 5 percent of their total donations to faith-based organizations. Foundations are just as biased with only 2 percent of the billions of dollars they give away going to religiously affiliated institutions, and much of that was earmarked for hospitals and universities.[3]

There was one major exception to the corporate disregard of the faith communities: Wal-Mart. This well-known company is a hero to some because of its efficiency and low prices. It is a negative force in the eyes of others because of the impact its huge stores make on local small businesses, the low wages of many of its employees, and its nonunion status. Yet the company, which is one of the largest and most successful in the United States, stands out from the crowd when it comes to corporate donations. Capital Research Center found that half the grants Wal-Mart provides go to a church or ministry.[4] In 2001 employees and customers of Wal-Mart Stores, Inc., raised and contributed $196 million to more than 100,000 organizations through the Wal-Mart Good Works community involvement program.[5]

According to the Wal-Mart website: "Wal-Mart founder, Sam Walton, believed in servant-leadership, which makes our mission to serve our Associates and customers with compassion and integrity. Our emphasis is on our Associates, children, families, the local community and other local programs that improve the quality of life in our communities."[6]

Wal-Mart's giving is focused on education, preservation of the environment and natural resources, and programs that benefit children. To further these aims, Wal-Mart giving is localized rather than conducted by headquarters. That ties its corporate donations to the needs of its local stores, their employees, and their communities.

Wal-Mart unashamedly includes faith-based organizations in its list of groups eligible for funding. The website says: "Churches— Our funding is directed to faith-based organizations that are conducting projects benefiting a broad section of the community."[7] Wal-Mart has made it a practice to fund the most effective programs—religious as well as secular—provided the projects benefit not only the members of the sponsoring organization but also the wider community. Wal-Mart's "Community Involvement Philosophy" states:

> We believe that community concerns are best addressed in our local communities. Our grassroots style of giving enables our Associates to identify and support organizations that are improving the quality of life right in their local communities. We empower our Associates to determine the best ways for our Stores, SAM'S CLUBS and Distribution Centers to be involved locally. Consequently, our stores, clubs and DC Associates in their own communities direct 100% of our funding initiatives. Wal-Mart's community involvement approach is a unique one. Associates combine financial and volunteer support to assist organizations in making a positive difference. Many of our community involvement programs require and encourage our Associates to be directly involved with community non-profit organizations and their projects. When we support

national causes, we require that funds stay in the local community
to benefit the area where they are raised.[8]

2. Some Corporate Foundations Do Not Support Faith-Based Programs

In contrast to Wal-Mart's exceptional giving pattern, the Capital
Research Center's survey shows that six of the nation's ten largest
businesses "ban or restrict donations to religious groups."[9] The
practices of AT&T stand in contrast to Wal-Mart's.

In 2001 AT&T worldwide contributed over $79 million to non-
profit organizations. More than $54 million was given in monetary
donations, and more than $25 million was given in products and
services. The AT&T website says that almost three-fourths of this
giving was initiated and driven by local managers responding to
needs of their local communities.[10]

Not all groups active in those local communities are eligible for
AT&T contributions, however. The grant guidelines for "AT&T
CARES" specifies that the following organizations cannot participate: "Organizations without 501(c)(3) public charity status
or organizations not registered with Revenue Canada's Charities
Division, for-profit organizations, *religious organizations,* and organizations engaged in political or lobbying activities" (emphasis
added).[11]

We should applaud AT&T's generosity and commitment to local
communities, but at the same time we should hold it accountable
for discriminating against faith-based service programs. The corporation encourages its employees to engage in community service
and then to advocate on behalf of their favorite organizations for
grant money. Yet according to its grant guidelines, if employees
recommend a faith-based organization for AT&T's support, they
will be turned down. Even faith-based groups that provide social
services not involving religious activities are ineligible for AT&T
CARES grants.

The Bank of America, on the other hand, will support faith-
based groups as long as the proposed project is not for "sectarian"
purposes. As the Bank's website says, faith-based organizations
provide "the building blocks your community needs, including
social, spiritual and developmental services."[12]

Sometimes the reluctance of corporations to support faith-based
organizations is attributed to the U.S. Constitution—supposedly

the requirement of the separation of church and state prevents businesses from donating to religious charities. That's nonsense of course. Corporations are not the "state"—they are not governments. Nobody is asking them to pay the preacher's or the rabbi's or the imam's salary, but instead they are being asked to support community-serving programs that are faith-based.

Still, large businesses have reason to be careful about the organizations to which they contribute. As Bob Buford says, "Public companies have a pluralistic point of view and probably should. Employees and stockholders come from multiple faiths. In many ways it's inappropriate for a public company to impose the faith of its executives on its shareholders or employees. Many corporate executives feel that tension. Probably it's like the difference between the Gates Foundation and Microsoft. Gates can allocate foundation money any way he wishes, where Microsoft probably can't."[13]

So it is understandable that a large company may be leery about funding programs that include inherently religious activities such as evangelism, worship, and Bible study. What sense does it make, though, for a corporation to disqualify a service organization simply because the organization has religious ties?

If the faith-based organization serves the needy without discrimination and *offers* rather than *forces* prayer and spiritual counsel, what makes it unworthy of broad public support? Furthermore, most faith-based programs, including those offered by congregations, do not require the needy to become believers in order to obtain help. As University of Pennsylvania professor Ram A. Cnaan reports, "The primary beneficiaries of the congregations' good works are needy children who aren't themselves members of the congregation that serves them. In Philadelphia, for example, a city with some 2,000 community-serving congregations, you can count on your fingers and toes the churches, synagogues and mosques that make services contingent on an expression of religious commitment."[14]

Moreover, faith-based services may achieve the same public good as the services provided by secular organizations and may well do so with greater efficiency and better results. Should they be ineligible simply because of their religious affiliation? As Tom McCallie, executive director of the Maclellan Foundation, asks, "Would corporate charities rather give money to groups that are less effective than faith-based organizations but are seen as less controversial?"[15] Unfortunately, in too many cases the answer is *yes.*

Strange, isn't it? Corporations need to be neutral—not hostile—toward the faith communities. AT&T does not disqualify customers or employees because of their religious affiliations; their faith commitments are not determinative of the service they are purchasing or rendering. Yet AT&T refuses even to consider a grant application from a faith-based organization. If AT&T wishes to truly represent their employees, shareholders, and customers, then they should allow *all* groups to compete for their grants. If they are concerned about the appearance of sectarianism, they can make a point of funding a range of groups.

Corporations that say they are committed to the best community services should not arbitrarily exclude faith-based groups from fair consideration for support. The ultimate result of banning faith-based providers is that some of the best services, closest to the needy and most trusted by them, will be left out of the picture, underfunded and unable to do all the good that they can do.

Wal-Mart and Bank of America have shown that corporations can support faith-based programs without ignoring good secular services and without promoting divisiveness or religious coercion. Their corporate good deeds are helping faith-based—and secular—groups expand their own good deeds. People who care about needy families and communities should applaud such corporations. The employees, trustees, and shareholders of corporations that arbitrarily exclude good faith-based providers, however, should work to change this counterproductive policy, and consumers might give thought to taking their business elsewhere.

3. Entrepreneurial Companies with a Personal Commitment to Faith-Based Services

Bob Buford comments that, although little corporate philanthropy flows to faith-based programs, as much as half of individual philanthropy does. Here the individual or family that founded the company is still identified with it and controls it. It's up to these owners, and not a separate foundation, to decide to whom to contribute and how much.

Will such personally directed companies give to church-based and parachurch social programs? Buford says that what's key is "finding business professionals who share a ministry's vision and passion."[16] That's not as automatic as you might think.

True, Buford says, the vast majority of Americans—and thus very many businesspeople—call themselves Christians. Yet only about 12 percent of Americans can be called committed Christians who attend church, pray, practice their faith, and give. About 28 percent are nominal Christians, who are active members of a church but are not deeply involved in praying, giving, and so on. Another 44 percent think of themselves as Christian (Protestant or Catholic) only because of their family history. The other 15 percent of the population belong to other religions, with just a few professed atheists. The most interesting point in all this, Buford points out, is that a study by George Gallup shows there are few real differences in behavior between the 28 percent and the 44 percent. (There is a similar situation in the Jewish community, Buford notes. About half of Jewish people are active believers and about half are non-practicing.)[17]

So if there is going to be increased support for church-based and parachurch ministries, it will most likely come from the 12 percent of the population who are committed Christians. In the case of the business sector, Buford says it means that support is most likely to come from privately owned or entrepreneurial companies where a strong individual makes the decisions. "That's where the power will come from—not from big public companies like General Motors."[18]

One of the shining examples of corporate philanthropy is the Maclellan Foundation. Thomas Maclellan immigrated to the booming industrial town of Chattanooga, Tennessee, in 1892, after immigrating to Nova Scotia from Scotland thirty years earlier. Although he was a man of modest means, his entrepreneurial spirit was strong and his discipline was steady. He believed that God's providence not only would lead him into a fruitful professional venture but would help him rebuild his life after professional misfortune.

Mr. Maclellan demonstrated that faith and vision when he bought half of Provident Life and Accident Insurance Companies, Inc. Provident was one of the first companies to offer insurance to its workers, securing well-being and financial provision for themselves and their families for the future. As a result, Provident flourished, as did the Maclellan family.

In 1945 the Maclellans formed a family foundation. Dora Maclellan Brown said, "The foundation of the Maclellan family has been truly Christian. It is the most valuable heritage we have to pass on to future leaders ministering under this name. . . . My own Christian experience has been so precious to me, I long to use my means in a way that will give this privilege to others."

Hugh O. Maclellan Jr. succeeded his father and assumed the role as the president of the Maclellan Foundation in 1994. Hugh is the third generation of his family to serve as president. Speaking on behalf of his family, Mr. Maclellan says that "the ultimate goal of the Maclellan Foundation in making grants and funding organizations is to fulfill The Great Commission."[19]

Today, the Maclellan Foundation supports more than two hundred ministries and charitable organizations each year. Its purpose is to serve strategic international and national organizations committed to furthering the kingdom of Christ and select local organizations that foster the spiritual welfare of the Chattanooga, Tennessee, area. The foundation serves by providing God's resources and godly leadership to extend the kingdom of God in accordance with the Great Commission.

COLLABORATING TO INCREASE EFFECTIVENESS

Even when an entrepreneurial business leader or corporate foundation knows the value of faith-based programs and wants to help support faith-based groups, it is still possible that no donations will be made. Why? Because the problem isn't prejudice or a false conception of constitutional limits; the problem lies in concerns about the competence and effectiveness of the faith-based groups.

Many corporations do not contribute to faith-based programs because the groups have the reputation of being well-meaning and passionate about their mission but lacking discipline and the capacity to be successful. In the words of one corporate foundation decision-maker, "Quite frankly, faith-based groups are a 'risky investment.' Their applications are sloppy, their vision is unclear, and there are no measured outcomes. The sad thing is that they can't see it."

In his landmark book, *Good to Great,* Jim Collins terms this internal blindness "dogs that did not bark." "In the Sherlock Holmes classic 'The Adventures of Silver Blaze,'" he writes, "Holmes identified 'the curious incident of the dog in the night-time' as the key clue. It turns out that the dog did nothing in the night-time and that, according to Holmes, was the curious incident that led him to the conclusion that the prime suspect must have been someone who knew the dog well."[20] Likewise, some faith-based organizations are so familiar with their mission and their practices that they cannot see where they are deficient. Collins contends that this internal blindness has some groups on life support when instead they should be conducting an autopsy to find out what needs to be changed.

"In the faith-based community, we tend to have a shotgun approach," observes Claudia Horn, president of Performance Results, a group that assists nonprofits with measuring program outcomes. "But you can't be everything to everybody. First step has to be to help a faith-based organization to examine what their program is all about. We try to help them answer three important questions in an 'elevator speech' format. In other words, in the time you would have in an elevator ride learn to be able to explain your program thoroughly. Be able to tell people we do (1) what, (2) for whom, (3) for what outcome or benefit. That defines the programs and the outcomes and the benefits to people."[21]

Although faith-based leaders may be worried that they aren't meeting all the needs they see, Collins warns that organizations are more endangered by dying from indigestion from too much opportunity than from starvation from too little. Congressional Medal of Honor recipient Admiral Jim Stockdale, who was the highest-ranking United States officer in the "Hanoi Hilton" prisoner of war camp during the Vietnam War, put it this way: "You must never confuse faith that you will prevail in the end—which you can never afford to lose—with the discipline to confront the most brutal facts of your current reality, whatever they may be."[22]

Leaders of faith-based groups who hope for support from the business sector need the courage to look hard at what their organizations are doing and how they are doing it. However, even the business community is uncertain about how to measure results. Horn says, "Businesses are asking for accountability but as of yet they just aren't sure what they are asking for." Horn contends that there is a misconception that evaluation should be about looking at process and how many people were served, while there's less of an emphasis on holding organizations to a standard of accountability. The corporations use the language of accountability but don't really know what results they would like to see from a program they are funding. "So faith-based organizations that want to be responsive don't know what to do to meet business leaders' expectations. So we need to move away from process—for example, saying just 'we had 212 hours of outreach'—and to the outcomes that resulted from that process."[23]

Confirmation about this lack of clarity comes from Harvard Business School professors Michael Porter and Mark Kramer in their study, *Giving Practices of American Foundations.* "Little effort is devoted to measuring results," they write. "On the contrary, foundations often consider measuring performance to be unrelated to their charitable mission."[24] Neither foundations nor corporations—whose bottom line is good service and profit—should be funding charities that do not achieve solid results.

Foundations, Porter and Kramer say, should create value "by funding the best and most effective grantees, attracting additional investment from other donors to the charitable cause or organization they are funding, improving performance of the grantee, and most important, advancing the knowledge of a field by paying for research."[25] This is the future, according to Horn: "Corporations are moving in the direction of outcomes very quickly. Not everyone is there yet, but there are some foundations that are beating this drum. Kellogg Foundation has been into outcomes for a long time."[26]

In addition to a concern with actual results and not just with activity, corporate America is increasingly interested in the financial practices of the groups to whom they give money. A sign of this emphasis is the controversy that has surrounded America's most well-known fundraising organization, the United Way. Stephanie Strom broke the story in a *New York Times* article in November 2001: "United Way organizations, trying to appear more successful and more efficient with their donors' money, are counting contributions in ways that make the numbers look more robust—and expenses look smaller."[27]

The article stated that two of the largest United Ways—Washington and Chicago—counted some of the same contributions even though they were different organizations, thus inflating not only their own numbers but the overall United Way income. While local United Ways publicly report the percentage of their total contributions used for administrative purposes, they do not disclose to donors that "different amounts are applied from different types of contributions to cover costs."[28]

In other words, the percentage of administrative costs may be much higher or lower for a specific donation than the percentage reported for total contributions. United Way's president said, "While some of the practices conformed with generally accepted accounting principles, they might no longer pass muster after recent corporate scandals demonstrated that even approved practices can be used deceptively."[29]

What conclusion should we draw from this? We believe that if faith-based groups are to successfully compete against secular organizations for corporate support, then our proposals, our mission statements, and our practices must be exemplary and set a lofty standard. For those corporate foundations that are already uneasy about supporting faith-based groups, a presentation or proposal that is less than the best will almost always tip the decision in favor of a group that is regarded as nonsectarian. In the corporate arena, good intentions are not good enough. Business leaders rightly want to know they are investing in efficient organizations that are going to achieve significant results.

Some faith-based organizations may consider these high standards to be a source of discouragement, a cause for complaint about obstacles blocking the way to resources for their good works. We believe, instead, that we should welcome the emphasis on outcomes and financial accountability. If we are serious about doing good in the name of Jesus Christ, then how can we be satisfied with less than the best effort?

Fortunately, business leaders not only want to set high standards for groups that turn to them for financial support but are often willing to invest themselves and their expertise in helping the groups achieve those high standards. Later in this chapter we will look at ways to build partnerships through which businessmen and women can help faith-based groups excel.

Businesses and Faith-Based Service Groups Need Each Other

Whatever the complications in their interrelationships, there is general agreement among faith-based and community-based organizations, corporations, and the government that collaboration is essential to meet the needs of our society. That is certainly the case in the linked areas of workforce preparation and welfare reform.

Consider these statistics: As baby boomers retire, the demand will grow for more and more replacement workers. "The Bureau of Labor Statistics projects that more than 17 million new jobs will be created between 1994 and 2005, but as the Hudson Institute Workforce 2020 report points out, that number will grow to 47.2 million once all vacated jobs (that is, jobs made available by retiring baby boomers) are included."[30] Nearly half of these jobs will be in medium- to high-skill occupations. Who will be ready to fill them?

One source of new workers is women and men who are moving from welfare to self-sufficiency. Welfare reform has been, in many ways, an amazing success story as hundreds of thousands of families have changed from dependency on handouts to being able to support themselves and their families. The percentage of people on welfare is now the lowest since 1967—a truly amazing fact, given that in 1994 the welfare rolls were at their highest level ever. Still, there is much more to be done.

On the one hand, as better-prepared adults have left welfare, those who remain are disproportionately the so-called "hard-to-employ." As the New York Times has reported, "As the willing and the capable have been prodded off public assistance, New York City officials say, they have left behind peers hobbled by addiction, disability and AIDS, a complaint that is increasingly voiced by welfare administrators across the country."[31]

In New York City over half of the welfare cases now include people "who meet the city definition of being capable of only limited work or no work at all. Even those able-bodied people still on the welfare rolls are increasingly likely to be illiterate or to stubbornly refuse work assignments despite fiscal penalties, city officials say. Since 1996, when the city began requiring able-bodied welfare recipients to work for their benefits, the number of people receiving public assistance has plummeted by more than two-thirds. Now, city officials say, comes the hard part."[32]

On the other hand, welfare reformers like President George W. Bush insist that we cannot stop with the changes that have been made this far. In 2002 the average state had about 30 percent of its welfare recipients working. The president and other defenders of the 1996 reforms insist that states should get to 50 percent by 2003 and 70 percent by 2007. They also want required hours at a job or training program to jump from 30 hours a week to 40.[33]

The heightened demands would be accompanied by federal funds for job training, drug rehabilitation, and education. "We are encouraged by the initial results of welfare reform, but we're not content," President Bush has said. "We ended welfare as we've known it, yet . . . child poverty is still too high. Too many families are strained and fragile and broken. Too many Americans still have not found work and the purpose it brings."[34]

The number of jobs will be expanding, and an increasing number of people will be coming off welfare and needing work. Yet many of those seeking jobs face enormous challenges in just coping with life and with their families. We could put the challenge this way: Who will prepare the former recipients of charity to become the new workforce?

One of the early lessons of welfare reform is that the best job training is an actual job, even if the work is at a low level. (Of course, if the head of a household remains stuck at that entry-level job, then she can hardly care adequately for her family, much less honor God and bless her neighbors with all her gifts. So attention also has to be given to career preparation and education.) There's a similar logic in the case of addictions. According to Teen Challenge, the successful faith-based drug and alcohol program, what is needed is to make sure that those hooked on drugs or alcohol do not merely sit around in intervention programs for years. The key is to engage recovering addicts as soon as possible in structured environments with meaningful work.

Who will provide those opportunities for people with little job experience, troubled backgrounds, and many burdens? Businesses, no matter how compassionate their leaders, cannot long operate as social ministries without concern for the financial bottom line. Corporations, not surprisingly, are reluctant to hire employees who are recovering from life-controlling problems and who lack the life skills to show up for work consistently and to perform well. A human resource director for a corporation (who asked to remain anonymous) said, "We have a duty to our shareholders to put the best workforce in place, and it is my responsibility when hiring people to consider the impact they will have on the workplace culture." Most of those who left welfare have found work, and yet many corporate leaders have been reticent to hire former welfare recipients because they lack the basic life skills to succeed at work. That is, employers are more concerned about "dependability and a strong work ethic than about formal education and work experience."[35]

Who, then, will help prepare the many who are not ready to show up regularly for work and those who need to kick their dependency on alcohol or drugs? Here is a natural avenue of service for faith-based organizations that believe in the dignity and capabilities of each person. Turning lives around is their mission—not just salvation but also changed habits and a renewal of personal responsibility. The challenge has been seen by some faith leaders, and they have been developing programs that work.

Amy Sherman, in her practical manual, *Establishing A Church-based Welfare-to-Work Mentoring Ministry*, states, "The old welfare system has been replaced with a new approach to poverty fighting that emphasizes hands-up instead of hand-outs. Welfare aid now aims to free recipients from dependency on it, and help them achieve greater economic self-sufficiency. This transition to independence from welfare frequently requires intense, personalized assistance that churches and ministries are well-positioned to provide."[36]

Success for such ministry requires "a faith-based organization working with an individual with no job [to] focus on such issues as work readiness skills, writing a resume, practicing job interviews, identifying potential job opportunities, making child care and transportation arrangements, etc."[37] Further, when the person takes a job, the faith-based ministry needs to anticipate potential problems that could jeopardize the employee's ability to retain her job.

JOBS PARTNERSHIP

Jobs Partnership is an outstanding example of a faith-based response to the challenge of preparing people to get and keep a job. Headquartered in Raleigh, North Carolina, its mission is "to bring churches and businesses together to mentor, train, and employ our country's neediest citizens, moving them from dependency to self-sufficiency as productive citizens of the community and to true wellness."[38]

Churches agree to work together and take on the mission to reach out to, mentor, and support each neighbor (person in need of work) that they sponsor through the Jobs Partnership. A neighbor is embraced by a local church, which works with him or her and provides all the help necessary to reach a place of financial self-sufficiency. For many, transportation, child care, and housing stand in the way and the church provides this assistance, calling upon the many, varied resources found within the local congregation to enable the neighbor to go forward. A personal mentor is assigned from the church to each student sponsored. The mentor's role is to provide assistance and accountability needed on a daily basis to help the student complete the training.

Local businesses also provide a key ingredient to the success of the program: *jobs.* Participating businesses agree to list their openings with the Jobs Partnership and seek to employ qualified graduates who are referred to them. Businesses also agree to provide employee benefits, training and advancement opportunity, and a mentor for on-the-job support and assistance. The business mentor or buddy helps the new employee make the transition into the workplace, providing answers to basic work-related questions.

In Raleigh, 93 percent of those women and men who have participated in the Jobs Partnership program since its inception in 1996 were still employed as of 2002, and the wage rates for those participants currently employed are as follows:

Percent of Total Participants	Wage Rates
30%	$7.50–$8.50
40%	$8.50–$10.00
30%	$10.00–$15.00

The collaboration yields benefits to the partners and community as well as to the individuals who have been helped into sustainable employment.

Benefits to the Business	Benefits to the Church	Benefits to the Community
Honest, reliable, hard-working employees to fill pressing needs in the company.	A vehicle for ministry, leading the people of the church into their community.	Enabling the most effective welfare program and thereby bringing true help to the unemployed: jobs.
Employees who have the support and guidance of their church sponsor.	Fulfilling Jesus' words, "Inasmuch as ye have done it unto one of the least of these my brethren, ye have done it unto Me" (Matt. 25:40).	Empowering people to become productive, taxpaying citizens who support their family and community.

SOURCE: Jobs Partnership, http://www.tjp.org (November 2002).

Jobs Partnership's success has resulted in collaborations with over one hundred businesses in the Raleigh area, and the program is now being duplicated nationwide. Jobs Partnership has developed collaborations with national companies such as Bank of America. Karen Shawcross, vice president of the Community Development Banking Group, said, "Because of our shared goals with the National Jobs Partnership of helping people to enter or re-enter the workforce and become self-sufficient, we have established this national partnership to work together in the communities we jointly serve. We have a shared mission of taking a holistic approach to knocking down the barriers that keep low-income individuals and families from moving from poverty to self-sufficiency."[39]

Skip Long, executive director of Jobs Partnership, adds: "I am excited that the National Jobs Partnership provides Bank of America the opportunity to connect with our neighbors in cities across America that are trying to rise up out of poverty. This new national strategic alliance with Bank of America also provides our neighbors with the resources to be able to take advantage of the opportunities provided by Bank of America to increase their skills and training to fill all of its positions that in the past have been hard to fill at Bank of America."[40]

Connie McWilliams, national outreach manager for personnel at Bank of America, said, "We look forward to deepening and developing new relationships between local Jobs Partnership programs and Bank of America Personnel offices as part of our overall strategy of building a powerful, effective and diverse workforce."[41]

When Long is asked how a faith-based organization such as Jobs Partnership can collaborate with a Bank of America, which disallows funds for sectarian purposes, he is quick to point out that "these classes aren't church. Students are given Bibles, yes, because the Bible is the course textbook, but they aren't required to believe it. Whether or not the big guy with the thick neck and the shaved head ever comes to Christ, the program will help him find work. Our role is just to love up on them, give them skills, help them get a job." Long explains, "Whether you're Muslim, atheist, Jewish—it's still unacceptable for you not to feed your family. Now, in my heart, do I want that the whole world would know? Yes. We have a biblical Christian worldview. That's who we are in this partnership, and we don't apologize at all. But how I operate now is God is calling me to love, period. And I've got to believe that the Word of God won't come back void."[42]

Building Fruitful Collaborations

Simply working with another group does not mean there is a true partnership. According to Suzanne Morse, executive director of Pew Partnership for Civic Change, working with others "requires that each collaborator understands the process and the product of their collaboration to make it work successfully."[43] If this is not understood from the outset, collaborations can be detrimental to all involved. The faith-based leadership should be clear about its calling and vision before entering into a partnership with a business. That doesn't mean that things will not change. It's quite natural that new ideas and projects might arise once a partnership gets going. Yet leaders of faith-based groups must not let collaboration lead to a forfeiture of their personal mission and calling.

Keys to Collaboration

As an Independent Sector report points out, collaboration between businesses, nonprofits, and governments will be successful when

- trust exists among partners and everyone is working for a common cause

- there is a shared vision and clear aim for a joint working arrangement
- there is a commitment among partners to make a difference
- all partners integrate expertise, ideas and information into operations
- there is open and honest communication
- individual partners leverage their strengths for the benefit of all organizations in the partnership[44]

Strategy for Collaboration

Research. Identify business leaders and corporations that have a track record of working with faith-based groups. We recommend that you begin with privately owned or entrepreneurial companies. Organizations such as Halftime, Fellowship of Christian Companies International, Christian Management Association, and the Christian Stewardship Association share the vision of empowering Christian nonprofits.

Relationship. Foster productive relationships with business leaders in your community through:

- inviting participants to tour your facility and observe your ministry
- hosting roundtable discussions with business and faith-based leaders
- conducting conferences and inviting business professionals to speak
- honoring business leaders for their contribution to the community by presenting them awards

Consider Bob Buford's word to corporate foundations, "Build long-term relationships that build organizational capacity and confidence, not 1 or 2 year programs only."[45]

Results. Many top corporate leaders are interested in finding real solutions to the systemic problems plaguing our communities. Therefore, find common ground on issues such as education, job training, health, and housing that your organization and the business can agree to target. Start with one project and then determine the kind of results (outcomes) you would like to see because of this new joint venture.

Resources. Develop a memo of understanding (MOU) that includes the roles and expectations for the faith-based group and corporation. In addition, agree on and assign the personnel, financial, and other resources needed to accomplish the mission. Buford cautions, "I want to back their ideas, to facilitate their success. We should hold the same mission in common but I don't want the [faith-based leaders] shaping a proposal to get my money and to be the carriers of my ideas."[46]

Report. Establish benchmarks with dates that you can monitor en route to the project's success. Furnish the business leaders with monthly reports that detail the progress, areas to improve, and any needs.

Reward. After the project is complete (or perhaps after the first year) jointly celebrate accomplishments and then promote the success to other corporate leaders.

What Government Can Do to Help

Building fruitful partnerships between religious charities and businesses is primarily the responsibility of the faith and business leaders. Yet government officials who want to promote expanded involvement of faith-based groups in services for the sake of greater effectiveness as well as fairness can take some steps to encourage these new partnerships.

1. *Government can serve as an effective connecter and convener of problem-solving coalitions.* Like no other institution, the government has the influence and platform to conjoin faith-based groups and corporations for roundtables, commissions, and projects that address our nation's problems. A great example is the Front Porch Alliance. In 1997, Mayor Stephen Goldsmith of Indianapolis launched the Front Porch Alliance to support and strengthen churches, neighborhood associations, and other community-based organizations. The Front Porch Alliance was a cooperative partnership between the city, faith institutions, neighborhoods, and community members to address local problems.

The Front Porch Alliance forged more than eight hundred partnerships, including more than four hundred religious and community organizations. The Alliance supports organizations that help needy families, provide activities for at-risk children, and promote community renewal. Since the Alliance was formed, more than twenty small businesses have moved into the west side of Indianapolis and more than two hundred homes have been built or refurbished. Crime rates plummeted, with homicides dropping by 70 percent, and seven hundred new jobs were created in the area. All this happened because a government official, Mayor Goldsmith, seized the potential of his public office to connect and coinvest with faith-based, community-based, and corporate institutions to create a problem-solving coalition.

2. *Government can minimize corporate fears by affirming the value of faith-based organizations.* Mac McQuiston, president of CEO Forum, a burgeoning alliance of corporate executives, said, "A lot would happen if we could convince the government or even the President to say to corporate leaders, 'Guys this is something you've got to do for the well-being of our culture and our country.' It will take some persuading, because they've been so ingrained that if I give to a Christian cause then I will have to give to a Muslim cause, or some other cause that doesn't match their beliefs and values. There are a lot of CEOs that might give to those causes but their Boards won't let them. It's a matter of persuading CEOs that have faith that they need to go back to their Boards and persuade them to say 'these FBO's [faith-based organizations] are much more effective."[47]

Both President George W. Bush and Jim Towey, head of the White House Office of Faith-Based and Community Initiatives, speak often to corporate and foundation leaders to encourage them not to overlook faith-based programs due to a mistaken view of church-state separation but instead to focus on results and on giving all effective groups a chance to win their support. In a speech to the Chamber of Commerce in Charlotte, North Carolina, in February 2002, President Bush thanked Charlotte and Mecklenburg County government, business, and faith leaders for developing an extensive collaboration to assist people to make the transition from welfare to sustained employment. Such partnerships in which the faith community plays a major role, the president said, were a key reason why welfare reform had worked, and such partnerships would be important in the further success of welfare reform.[48]

3. *Government can affirm the value of faith-based organizations by investing public funds to promote corporate/faith-based partnerships.* We saw in chapter

3 that an important element in President Bush's strategy to "rally the armies of compassion" is policy changes that will encourage an outpouring of private individual and corporate giving to faith-based and secular charities. In 2001 and 2002 both the House and the Senate worked to pass legislation to make those changes, although the efforts did not succeed. Furthermore, a number of states or localities have contracted with the Jobs Partnership to build local collaborations that bring together faith-based groups with businesses to train and place the unemployed in long-term jobs.

THE VISION THING

America desperately needs public/private partnerships so that work across racial, denominational, urban/suburban, and other divides can achieve lasting results. America is calling for public officials to work overtime and in a bipartisan fashion to ensure "that the social programs taxpayers fund, and the networks of nonprofit organizations that help to administer those programs, are performance-managed, performance-measured, and open to competition from qualified community-serving organizations, large or small, young or old, sacred or secular."[49]

The climate has never been more promising for the religious and corporate communities to build problem-solving relationships that transcend politics and corporate fears. A fitting conclusion to this chapter are comments from Mac McQuiston and Bob Buford, who have been leading stalwarts in fostering corporate and faith-based partnerships.

McQuiston: "There has to be a vision created on the part of faith-based groups that will capture the imagination of a corporation. Not only the vision, but what the influence is going to be on a given issue if that corporation joins that faith-based group's work. [These corporate leaders] don't lack for places to give, but they want to know that where they give, they are getting the most for their dollar."[50]

Buford: "This is a very personal enterprise. A calling is personal. God doesn't call foundations. He calls individuals. The responsibility is personal. The money and the organization are an extension of the person. They enlarge personal capacity. I want to facilitate what is trying to happen, what is going to happen anyway whether I'm involved or not."[51]

5

Collaborating
with the Social Sector

*Tommy Thompson [Federal Health and Human Ser-
vices Secretary] has said that government can't handle
this crisis alone. Long after the government's disaster
teams and aid workers have left New York City and the
Pentagon, the churches, synagogues, and mosques will be
there to help people pick up and carry on with their lives.
How government can help that assistance be more effective is one of the topics being discussed at the summit.*

   *Sitting alongside the representatives from faith groups
at the summit will be secular mental-health providers. In
the past, many of these providers, such as the National
Association of Social Workers, have loudly and defiantly*

challenged the notion that faith-based groups should play
a significant part in service delivery.

But a lot has changed since September 11.

—excerpt from "When Terror Strikes:
Responding to the Nation's Mental
Health and Substance Abuse Needs,"
GovExec.com, 16 November 2001

Americans are volunteers more than citizens of any other nation, helping their neighbors, donating time, money, and expertise. We do this either by lending a hand ourselves or by supporting any of hundreds of thousands of nonprofit service organizations, and our nation depends on those organizations. When there is a disaster, when a family is in crisis, when a child is sliding toward delinquency, we expect not only the government but also our thriving social sector to step in. We also expect the government to work in partnership with private groups.

Our social safety net, as we saw in chapter 2, has always been like this—composed of private groups, government programs, and partnerships between government programs and private programs. Religious social ministries have always been part of the social safety net, too, playing their part in the social sector. In fact, large national networks like the Salvation Army, Catholic Charities, Lutheran Services of America, and the United Jewish Communities constitute a major and vital part of America's safety net, and they have long worked with government and with other social organizations.

However, when our nation responds to disasters, the process of coordinating public/private networks of services often leaves churches and smaller faith-based groups on the outside looking in. Even when they are included, the established religiously affiliated organizations in the partnerships have been constantly pressured to downplay or entirely set aside their faith character.

How can a nation's compassionate response to need neglect the resources of faith? We need a Revolution of Compassion that enlists all the forces available to minister to "the least, the last, and the lost," in John DiIulio's words. Fortunately, change has begun, including rather than excluding faith-based groups in networks of care and response. Change has begun, valuing faith-based organizations *because* they are faith-based. Change has also begun within some of the traditional religious social agencies, as they fight back to recover and express their holistic mission of service to souls as well as bodies.

In this chapter we will see both the promise of effective compassion when faith-based resources are included and the tragedy of excluding them. We will also see how the Salvation Army, as a religious organization, has wrestled with energy and persistence to be a full partner in our nation's coordinated networks of care and response. If evangelical Christians want the world to see what we work *for* and not just what we stand *against,* we will have to be more active participants in the social safety net. We cannot afford to remain aloof for the sake of purity. Nor can we abandon our convictions for the sake of partnership.

Bad News, Good News in New York City

Thank God for the immediate and heartfelt response to the tragic events of 9/11 in New York City. Firefighters and rescue workers rushed to the scene and into the burning skyscrapers at Ground Zero. The Red Cross rolled into action. FEMA—the Federal Emergency Management Agency—activated its response teams and alerted its local partners. In the hours, days, and weeks that followed the tragedy, the federal Department of Health and Human Services worked with local hospitals, large corporations worked with small businesses, official national charities worked with neighborhoods. Vast shipments of donated resources and massive amounts of money quickly began flowing to the disaster area and were put to work.

Armies of compassionate people hurried to Ground Zero to assist FEMA, the Red Cross, the firefighters, and the police in responding to the victims and their families. FEMA and the Red Cross established a Family Center to offer information to the families of the victims as well as counseling services provided by professional counselors and psychiatrists brought in by the government.

Others rushed to help, too, but their efforts were rejected. For example, when more than seven hundred pastors came to offer help

Against and For

The words are still ringing in my ears, "You are known more for what you are against than what you are for."

In the spring of 1997, President Bill Clinton and former presidents Jimmy Carter, Gerald Ford, and George Bush had joined forces with Colin Powell, then chairman of America's Promise, to launch the Presidents' Summit for America's Future in Philadelphia, Pennsylvania. Social groups, nonprofit organizations, and corporations would be challenged to mobilize volunteers and offer equipment and expertise in a sustained outreach to America's disadvantaged youth.

"What a wonderful opportunity," I (Dave) thought, "to show the nation how different groups can work together to serve the poor." I envisioned this becoming an annual catalyst that would inspire sustained partnerships between faith-based groups, corporations, and social-sector organizations like the Red Cross, Goodwill, and the YMCA. I was encouraged that President Clinton and General Powell wanted to celebrate community service and highlight the diversity, innovation, and effectiveness of volunteerism in America.

My exuberance was greatly dampened, though, when

I saw the invitation list to the Summit. To my chagrin, not many Christian groups were invited, and even fewer evangelical faith-based ministries.

I decided to meet with one of the coordinators of the event to find out what was going on. I asked him, "Why are 60 million American evangelicals hardly represented at the Presidents' Summit for America's Future?"

His response was shocking: "I looked at the list of potential invitees and I thought, these church groups are known more for what they are against than what they are for. I didn't invite you because I thought you wouldn't care."

at the Family Center, they were turned away. They did not have credentials acceptable to the emergency managers. Exclaimed one of the pastors, "I've been working in this city for more than twenty years, and a teenage volunteer for the American Red Cross tells me I can't minister to these people!"

In the meantime, many who came to the Family Center hoping for assistance did not find what they were looking for. One eyewitness said, "When the families arrived seeking help, they didn't want to talk with a psychiatrist! They wanted to speak with a pastor, priest, or rabbi." This was verified by another observer who told We Care America, "I walked to a back room and the psychiatrists were playing cards because no one wanted to see them."

What a terrible tragedy, compounding the pain and horror already caused by the terrorists. The problem, however, wasn't just about helpful clergy being arbitrarily turned away. The officials in charge of the disaster response system simply could not allow everyone who showed up professing good intentions access

"This might be your perception," I responded, "but we do care! We care about America."

Still he shook his head, saying, "It's difficult for me to really believe that. What I see in the midst of growing poverty isn't an outpouring of service. Instead, I see churches building bigger and more grandiose buildings, and tele-evangelists fleecing their flocks."

As I left his office later, I tried to shake off his comments. He just doesn't know us. He isn't aware of all of the great work our churches do in cities across the nation. Maybe he has some hidden hurt toward the church that has made him so calloused toward us. Still, despite my rationalization, I knew the man's words carried an element of truth.

We evangelical Christians are known for our opposition to abortion, homosexual practice, and divorce, and for that we do not apologize. However, obedience to God's Word also requires of us compassion for the hurting and a commitment to restoring lives and communities. How many people know that we are not just against abortion, but also for adoption as an alternative and for helping women who have had abortions piece their lives back together again? Do they know that we aren't against homosexuals at all but are for seeing them set free from hidden guilt and bondage? Do they know that we are not only against divorce but for happy marriages, impassioned about seeing marriages restored, and also for helping divorced people cope with the pain of rejection?

If many Americans, like the government official who was helping to coordinate the Presidents' Summit for America's Future, know only the things we oppose and not our actions of service, is that because they are biased? Could it be because our service is too limited or too hidden? Or is it a little of each?

to the families and the Family Center. Additional terrorists might well have entered the scene of devastation by putting on clerical collars. Well-meaning but untrained people might have harmed rather than helped the families, adding more fuel to the emotionally explosive situation.

Still, it wasn't right for capable ministers and ministries to be excluded. The pastors who were turned away had brought with them the goodwill, resources, and social capital of their respective congregations, their denominational affiliation, and their communities. Many were trained in the delivery of critical incident management and counseling; all were experienced in working personally with broken people. Whatever their qualifications, they were excluded because they had not been afforded recognized advance training or credentialing.

The underlying problem was—and continues to be—the decades-long marginalization of many Christian organizations from the federal, state, and local disaster and emergency response systems. These systems are composed of officials and networks responsible for recruiting, training, approving, and coordinating organizations, staff, and volunteers to provide quick, effective, and expert assistance in the event of major tragedies. Of course, coordination is right. Training is essential. Certification or credentialing of trained and approved workers and groups is an important way to ensure that "help" doesn't make things worse. Yet the marginalization of faith-based leaders and groups from crisis response systems is wrong in principle, wasting valuable resources and goodwill, delaying and impoverishing relief efforts.

Naturally, churches and ministries find other ways to provide help, separate from the official response system, but this is not the most effective way for them to assist. As Mark Publow, a former national director for World Vision, told us, "When the only way for thousands of faith-based workers and organizations to respond to disaster is through spontaneous or convergent volunteerism, the outcome will work against both effective volunteerism and the effective management of crisis."

Most emergency planners see little value in unorganized voluntary assistance that arrives on its own schedule, but there is no process in place to prepare the hundreds and thousands of believers and faith-based groups who want to help. There is also no comprehensive system to communicate with them and organize their response. This is why their contribution is seldom fully utilized. Perhaps saddest of all, according to the Red Cross in Oklahoma City, many of these volunteers are lost to future volunteer efforts because of negative or emotionally harmful experiences during their spontaneous effort to help.

One regional emergency planner told us: "There is a big void in emergency planning that relates to the faith community. But most emergency planners are unaware of this resource, so it is underutilized."

How could emergency planners be unaware of the faith community? There are hundreds of thousands of congregations and parachurch ministries that exist in our nation, several in every neighborhood, in each rural town. In fact, all too often in our inner cities hardly anyone else but the faith community is working.

On the other hand, how aware are evangelical Christians (or other conservative people of faith) that each community, state, and region has response systems that unite government and private organizations in a coordinated network? Yes, it's true that many Christian organizations are marginal to these systems. But why? Perhaps, at least to some extent, this happens because of our own tendency to turn inward, to think only of cooperating with like-minded groups, and to regard government and public/private partnerships as threatening, ineffective, or even counterproductive. Perhaps part of the solution is for us to prayerfully rethink how our ministries of mercy, our programs, and our people relate to other groups. How good are we at interfacing with government, secular groups, and other religious nonprofit service efforts?

SERVING THE PUBLIC: THE SALVATION ARMY'S CHALLENGES AND SUCCESSES

Although those hundreds of pastors who arrived at Ground Zero in New York found their offers of help spurned by the officials who ran the organized disaster response effort, not all faith-based groups were excluded. In fact, the Salvation Army was deeply involved in that response—an indispensable partner in the coordinated network of response organizations.

Access and a prominent role for the Salvation Army at Ground Zero in New York City should come as no surprise. The Salvation Army has a long history of responding to victims of disasters, beginning with the San Francisco Earthquake in 1906. Throughout the Depression and World War I and II, the government's dependence on the Salvation Army for disaster relief services grew significantly. Over the years the Army has developed a strong collaboration with the American Red Cross and with FEMA. Also, a representative of the Salvation Army serves on the board of the National Emergency Food and Shelter Program, which is administered by the United Way and governed by FEMA.

The Salvation Army has blazed a trail that other faith-based ministries should follow if they want to be included in the coordinated response to disaster, if they want to gain routine access to victims and their families, and if they want to maximize opportunities.

The Salvation Army was founded as an evangelistic organization. It is currently the most prominent evangelical faith-based charity that delivers social services in partnership with the government and with secular organizations. Yet there are conservative believers who dismiss the Salvation Army as compromised in its Christian witness. "If the Army has blazed the trail," they say dismissively, "then maybe other faith-based groups need to follow another trail."

The Salvation Army has, in truth, had its ups and downs. Like other religious organizations that pioneered collaboration with government during the decades when the reigning interpretation of the First Amendment was no-aid separationism, it has often faced skeptical officials who welcomed its participation but found its religious character troublesome and dispensable. However, the Army has tenaciously maintained its faith basis and its insistence on ministering to hearts as well as bodies.

Today, as overly restrictive rules have started to be loosened by government officials, the Salvation Army has had the opportunity to give fresh content to its ministries. Churches and parachurch ministries can learn a lot by looking at the Army's challenges and successes. They can gain valuable insight from its relations with government, with secular social service organizations, and with a public interested more in the Army's social services than in its message of salvation. Because of the Salvation Army's unique history, we will focus on their mission, their ministry, and their implicit message to other faith-based organizations.

The Mission of the Salvation Army

Nowadays, when most Americans think of the Salvation Army, they envision Christmas bell ringers and thrift shops, neither of which seems particularly dedicated to faith and evangelism. In fact, many of us do not think of the Salvation Army as a devoutly Christian religious movement. Instead, it is seen as a well-respected, large national social services operation. Speaking to a group of religious leaders, I (Dave) once asked, "How many think the Salvation Army is an evangelical-Protestant ministry?" Less than half raised their hands. I went on to ask, "How many think the Salvation Army is a good example of a Christian ministry providing social services while maintaining its evangelistic mission?" A little more than a quarter of the crowd raised their hands.

So what is the story? Is the Salvation Army devoted to evangelism? Or is it committed to social services? Or does it try to do both? William Booth, the Army's founder, summed up its mission this way: "My only hope for the permanent deliverance of mankind from misery, either in this world or the next, is the regeneration or remaking of the individual by the power of the Holy Ghost through Jesus Christ. But in providing for the relief of temporal misery, I reckon that I am only making it easy where it is now difficult and possible where it is now all but impossible, for men and women to find their way to the cross of our Lord Jesus Christ."[1]

At its Centennial Celebration in 1991, the Salvation Army reissued this mission statement: "The Salvation Army, an international movement, is an evangelical part of the universal Christian Church. Its mission is to preach the gospel of Jesus Christ and to meet needs in His name without discrimination."[2]

In its own eyes, the Salvation Army is dedicated to evangelism and to social services. It does both in the name of Jesus. Yet its very popularity has become a two-edged sword. As Charles Glenn states in his study *The Ambiguous Embrace: Government and Faith-based Schools and Social Agencies,* "Even the most ardent Salvationist would acknowledge that the Army's popularity with the public and government funders has not been without cost."[3]

On one hand, that popularity has provided a fertile soil for marketing and fundraising efforts. On the other, the "Salvation" in the organization's name continues to fade from the general public's consciousness. Has the Army's mission and zeal for winning souls taken a backseat to meeting material needs? Or has the high visibility of its social programs merely overshadowed its evangelistic efforts?

Dual Ministries

Lt. Colonel Paul Bollwahn, the Salvation Army's national secretary for social services, points out that William Booth started his ministry with a single mission: to proclaim the gospel of Christ for the salvation of souls.[4] Much of England at the time was impoverished, and since Booth thought that was just the way things were, his social conscience was not particularly ignited early in his ministry.

As Booth later pointed out, at the start of his ministry he didn't see any remedy for poverty, so his early passion for the needy was expressed in his itinerant preaching and personal evangelism. However, his commitment to God, his love for all to whom he preached, and his genuine sensitivity toward the poor sparked in him a social imperative. Experiencing poverty himself was a profound education, Booth later said.

As the Salvation Army matured, many of those within its ranks "began to recognize the complexity of their ministry, and there dawned an awareness . . . that it was not enough to preach the Gospel to the poor, but that preaching had to be complemented by taking care of the physical needs of the poor to whom they preached."[5] Not all agreed. In fact, Booth's wife, Catherine, and George Scott Railton, two of his closest colleagues, "were adamant that the primary work of the ministry—the chief work of the Christian Mission and the Salvation Army—was the conversion of sinners and the raising up of saints."[6]

Yet it was increasingly clear to Booth and his followers that "one could not minister to the soul and ignore either the health of the body or the effects and relationships of the social environment. To do so would be to ignore dimensions of life that God Himself had created."[7] Thus, Salvation Army social work expressions began in various locations throughout the world: A rescue home for women opened its doors in Glasgow, Scotland, May 1883; a halfway house for released prisoners was started in Melbourne, Australia, December 1883; a rescue home for prostitutes was launched in the Whitechapel section of London, May 1884; a treatment center for women alcoholics began operations in Canada in 1886; a child day care center was set up in one of the slum ports of London in 1887.

"These ministries were not initiated as a result of theological study," one author has pointed out; instead, "they were concrete expressions of that theology of the burning heart which was the real operative theology of Salvationists." In other words, as they pursued their "evangelical mission to the poor and oppressed" they came to see that "God had created human life in many dimensions, and that redemption, in order to be complete, must touch upon all of them."[8]

Following Jesus

Paul Bollwahn emphasizes that it is the Salvation Army's conviction that ministry to the whole person is what the Bible commands and is what Jesus modeled.

- Jesus started his public ministry by meeting social needs: He provided drink at the marriage at Cana (John 2:1–11), healed the nobleman's son (John 4:46–54), healed the paralyzed man by the pool of Bethesda (John 5:1–9), and fed the five thousand (John 6:11). He set an example for servanthood by washing the disciples' feet (John 13:1–9) and showed compassion by healing those who were sick and demon-possessed (Mark 1:23–42).
- Jesus preached and practiced true religion that involves service to those in need: He acknowledged a call to preach to the poor, to liberate the oppressed, to heal the sick and brokenhearted, and to proclaim a time of reconciliation with God and freedom from the results of human sin (Luke 4:18).
- Jesus practiced holistic healing without distinction: He responded to the ignited faith of a social outcast with the same compassion as he did to a nobleman's sick boy and a man physically handicapped for thirty-eight years. Believers resulted from his comprehensive healing ministry (John 4–5).
- Jesus practiced advocacy for those in need of social justice: He came as a servant to all and stood for justice (Matt. 12:18); he showed the consequence of social injustice (Luke 16:19–31).
- Jesus also practiced giving from a heart dedicated to God without a required response: In the Sermon on the Mount, Jesus told his disciples to love, do good, and lend without expecting return (Luke 6:35–38).

This imperative not to neglect the physical needs of others is also emphasized elsewhere in the New Testament. For example, as Bollwahn notes, James declares that saving faith must be accompanied by action (James 2:14–17) and that acting in faith is redemptive (James 2:25). Saints are admonished in 1 John 3:18 to love not "with words or tongue but with actions and in truth." Salvationists, who are in the Wesleyan tradition, particularly note that those who were filled with the Holy Spirit on the day of Pentecost rejoiced and shared verbal praise but also involved themselves in practical giving to those in need (Acts 2:42–47; 4:32–35).[9]

In the Salvation Army, social ministry was never intended to replace sharing the Good News. Yet over the years that commitment to spreading the gospel has sometimes seemed to be overshadowed. "Although the Army remained committed to evangelism, its overt religious activities began to decline during the fifties and sixties. Between 1950 and 1965, the number of street meetings fell by almost 50 percent, and by 1980 the Army conducted just one-tenth as many outdoor evangelistic meetings as it had in 1950."[10]

Pressured by Government Requirements

Some have said that all government money is tainted with sin. According to Bollwahn, William Booth liked to say, "The only problem with tainted money is that it 'tain't enough.'"[11] In Booth's view, the world's tainted money was washed clean in God's service to the poor. As he enlarged his concept of biblical service, from evangelism alone to the gospel *and* social uplift, he sought a broader constituency, reaching out beyond his early supporters to nondenominational evangelical societies, then to the secular public in general, and eventually to the government.

Government money permitted expanded social services. Paul Bollwahn points out, "The more people you help, the healthier your neighborhoods, schools, churches and this nation will be." Yet government funding also brought pressure to de-emphasize evangelism. While the Salvation Army "manages to keep religion close at hand as it helps the needy," nevertheless, "it must push explicit expressions of faith to the periphery."[12]

Witness and worship are parts of the Salvation Army's outreach to the needy, but in government-funded programs, spiritual activities are separated from social services. For example, Bible study is offered, but only after the tutoring session is over. The government provides funds for the tutoring, while the Army pays for the Bible study. Clients receiving social services during the week are encouraged to attend the Army's church on Sunday; on Sunday the parishioners are reminded about the social services available during the week.

The Army's Faith-based Counseling Skills manual advises counselors to wait patiently for the right opportunity, perhaps after several sessions, to introduce scriptural references or to ask to pray with a client. When providing a meal paid for with public funds, Army officers perform devotionals after the meal, so their guests do not feel it is a prerequisite to receiving the meal. People are invited to remain afterwards for the devotion only if they wish to do so.

In the eyes of some people, both inside and outside the Salvation Army, such requirements mean there is not much difference between what the Army does and what secular nonprofits do, except for some religious extras tacked on to the social services.[13] Others have seen this division of activities as a reasonable accommodation to the diverse clientele the Army's programs serve and to the government's need not to appear to be endorsing any particular religion.

Anyone who comes to the Salvation Army for services is unquestionably being served by a faith-based organization that is concerned not only for their external behavior but also for their spiritual condition. Yet, over time, the strong emphasis on expert social services has tended to overshadow the Army's fundamental nature as an evangelical church. Under the restrictive rules of church-state separation, government officials prized the Salvation Army because of its efficient and effective provision of services, without honoring or valuing its faith-based character. In the same way, the public, contributing coins and bills to the Christmastime Salvation Army kettles and larger donations to other fund drives, valued the Army for its compassionate service. They did not much care to be reminded about the One who motivated that service. Under such pressures, Bollwahn noted, "The biblical five-fold Mission of the Church—Worship, Evangelism, Education, Fellowship, and Service—can easily be segmented into competing missions, if we lose perspective."[14]

A Seamless Ministry

Faith-based ministries are not at the mercy of the government or the public unless they allow themselves to be. They follow a greater

Master and can push back against external pressures. In reflecting on the ways its social ministry has complemented or overshadowed its gospel ministry, the Salvation Army has worked to develop a stronger overall vision of ministry. Former general Paul A. Rader called it the vision of a "seamless ministry."

What this requires, Bollwahn says, is not for the Army to drop one or another of its dual callings but rather to find a way to make sure they are both emphasized, as they were in Jesus' own life and work. Each member of the body, whether working at social services or at worship and evangelism, must work in complete faithfulness and in coordination with the others. In that way, "whether planting or watering (1 Cor. 3:3–8), we can witness the effect planned by Christ, the author of our faith and sustainer of our movement."[15]

Salvation Army workers are all familiar with the phrase, "We are saved to serve." In discipling new converts, their involvement in social ministry is as important as their learning how to share their newfound faith. Serving is important to growing in the nurture of Jesus *and* in the grooming of spiritual leaders. In Bollwahn's words, "Salvationists believe that we are saved not only to enjoy our new life and to talk about it, but to do something with the new power and the benefits received. Indeed, it is through a perspective of seeing beyond ourselves that we fulfill the plan of salvation by extending to those in need a hand of service, fellowship and inclusion, assuming them to be potential in Christ's Kingdom equal to our own."[16]

Christians should not divide the *ministry* of the church into segmented *ministries,* Bollwahn concludes. Rather, it is our responsibility as the body of Christ to work under the guidance of the Holy Spirit, according to Scripture, toward "holism" through the equal emphasis of each facet of the biblical fivefold *mission.*

Pushing Back

Many in the Salvation Army have watched with anticipation Congress's adoption of Charitable Choice and the actions of President George W. Bush and other leaders to advance the faith-based initiative. It is not that the Army requires policy change in order to be able to win government funding for some of its social services. What is important for the Salvation Army is a change in government policy and attitudes so that the Army is free to express its character as a faith-based organization that believes people need not only services but also the gospel.[17]

As government's respect for faith-based programs gains ground, the Army has been at work itself to oppose the tendencies that elevate its social services above its gospel witness. One major way has been to engage in intensive discussions over the past few years about its dual missions: How should they reinforce instead of undermine each other?

The Army has also reexamined its policies about accepting government funds. It has never accepted a very large part of its income from government. It believes, instead, that government funds should be *supplemental* to other income, preserving the Army's independence and its ability to carry on programs—even if the government funding dries up. Currently only about 15 percent of the Army's funding is from government programs. About 7 percent is from the United Way. The rest of the income is from donations.

Yet even a relatively small amount of money from government sources can draw a faith-based group away from its full mission if the rules that come with the money are incompatible with that mission. Salvation Army officials have been reconsidering the different conditions that accompany various government-funding programs. Their willingness to close down programs that are incompatible with their calling is reflected in their closure of the William Booth Hospital in Flushing, New York. The hospital "over time had become just like any other well-run, successful hospital . . . a respectable institution and a worthy cause, but not the vision of William Booth!"[18]

To make sure its ministry really is seamless, the Army has also been giving renewed attention to its employment standards. Who carries out a ministry makes all the difference in what that ministry actually is. As William Booth said, "All the social activity of the Army is the outcome of the spiritual life of its members. All social service must be based on the spiritual or it will amount to little in the end."[19]

Sometimes government contracts and grants come with the requirement that the recipient organization must ignore religion when hiring and firing staff. Because organizations can ask that employees fit in with the organization, the rule about no religious staffing does not inevitably mean that Catholic or Jewish or other groups that take government funds end up filled with staff who disregard faith. Still, this view that it is illegal and somehow immoral for a faith-based organization to be concerned about the faith commitments of the people who direct it and work for it is a threat to the religious character of the organization and may expose it to lawsuits.

Of course, people aren't immoral or incompetent or uncompassionate just because they are not Bible believers. Sad to say, a confession of faith is no guarantee, either, of an upright life. Yet it is hard to understand how social services can fully mesh with a gospel witness if those who provide the social services are not committed to the gospel themselves.

Ending up with a staff that isn't deeply devoted to a faith mission is not a problem caused simply by government funds. A bigger cause is professionalization. As social service groups like the Salvation Army expand their social programs, they need staff who are qualified to provide specialized services and to manage their programs. This need can create a tendency to focus on professional credentials more than spiritual commitment.

Let's be clear: Government policy concerning hiring faith-based organizations needs to be reformed. Why should Planned Parenthood be able to refuse to hire pro-lifers when faith-based organizations that agree to collaborate with government may be pressured to hire staff without regard to religious convictions? Still, the issue of professionalization may be more challenging than present hiring restrictions.

Being an expert social worker should not be in conflict with being a follower of Jesus; rather, love of God should be reflected in effective help for the needy. Yet conventional professional training too often neglects or even looks down on Christian belief. Sadly, evangelical Christians in turn too often have looked down on professions such as social work and counseling.[20]

For the Salvation Army and other faith-based organizations to be fully able to fulfill William Booth's emphasis on the "spiritual life" of staff members, government officials need to reform rules that unjustly hamper faith-based hiring. At the same time, faith needs to become an integral part of professional training. Finally, the evangelical community needs to hold out social service as a God-honoring career choice.

Domestic Partners

Because Salvation Army units are located throughout the nation, and large cities increasingly are promoting pro-gay policies, the Army has faced hard decisions and received much criticism about providing domestic partner benefits to employees. Some city governments require all contractors to offer such benefits or else they must give up their government funding to support their social services.

This issue is not a simple one of being faithful or being funded, as a Salvation Army publication argues. Offering domestic partner benefits does not imply an endorsement of the gay lifestyle. On the other hand, however, "refusing to provide benefits to an employee's gay partner will most certainly serve to alienate Christian ministries further from gays in general, and will confirm the widespread perception that Christians 'hate' gays."[21]

What should Christian ministries do, the policy document argues, if—despite the movement to make government rules less restrictive to faith-based ministries—more and more cities make all contractors provide domestic partners benefits? Then "it is clear that by not providing these benefits, there would be a significant loss of faith-based groups' ability to minister to people in Christ's name. We would be abandoning a sizeable part of the mission field God has given us; we would be abandoning a significant number of people, and many of the agencies that would take over those services would not represent Christ and would have no spiritual ministry."[22]

Faithfulness, it turns out, is more than successfully fighting off the temptation to accept government money. It must also somehow take in both purity of mission and the actual giving of help to people who need the help.

CATHOLIC CHARITIES

Catholic Charities rivals the Salvation Army as a provider of extensive and cost-effective social services. Despite its roots in and connections with the Roman Catholic Church, it sees itself not so much as a faith-based organization but as a "service agency," delivering professionalized services. Sharon Daly, vice-president for social policy for Catholic Charities USA, has said, "The primary role of Catholic Charity agencies is helping people, rather than teaching them any particular religious belief."[23] Some two-thirds of its annual income is from federal, state, or local governments—a far higher percentage than for the Salvation Army.

Given all this, many—and not only evangelicals—have wondered whether Catholic Charities should even be called a faith-based social service provider. Not long ago the late Cardinal John O'Connor delivered a stinging homily to charity officials at New York's St. Patrick's Cathedral. He supported their work, he said, but he saw a "creeping dependence" on government funding, caused by the need to follow "the requirements of government regulatory procedures." "With dependence on government funding," O'Connor warned, "always we must expect governmental control."[24]

In 1997, U.S. Senator Rick Santorum (Pennsylvania), a devout Catholic, sharply condemned Catholic Charities for becoming too much like a secular service organization because of its dependency on government funding. "They can do little that is uniquely Catholic," he said. "They have to do what the government dictates, which means they can't talk about the *Catholic* part of the charity." And he asked, "How can we have allowed the welfare state to co-opt our institutions in the Catholic Church?"[25]

Fortunately, concerns about the spiritual direction of this very large service agency are not only external, although the tendency to downplay faith and stress expert services is very strong. The passage of Charitable Choice, President Bush's faith-based initiative, and the success of welfare reform along with other factors have led to some soul searching that we should all applaud and encourage. Three years of internal discussions about the direction of Catholic Charities resulted in the Vision 2000 statement. "The Church's social teaching and the mission of Catholic Charities call us to do more than acts of charity, more than delivering services through a variety of programs," the statement said. "The Church's works of mercy and its ministries of service must witness to the faith of the entire Church and live out our baptismal anointing."[26]

To that we can only add, "Amen."

STRENGTHENING THE SOCIAL SAFETY NET

There always will be both natural and man-made disasters of all types. There will continue to be despair and disruption caused by poverty, crime, family breakdown, and other social ills. In the past, natural disasters such as earthquakes, hurricanes, tornadoes, and floods have significantly affected our nation's economy and have had a devastating impact on the individuals and families directly affected. Man-made catastrophes such as fires, hazardous materials incidents, and acts of terrorism have increasingly played a role in our nation's emergency response planning.

These calamities not only have an immediate impact but leave a lasting mark on the families and communities involved. According to those who cared for both victims' families and workers in Oklahoma City after the terrorist bombing there, an increase in family disruption, depression, and suicide occurred in the years that followed. More than a quarter of the families affected still need services more than six years later.

Restoring families and communities devastated by disaster requires more than generic counseling or case management, and the care may need to be sustained for ten years or more. This level of care requires the full engagement of the churches and other religious institutions that are an integral part of every community. As Ronald Reagan once said, "No government caseworker can restore a broken spirit." The power required to minister to body, soul, and spirit can be found only in America's faith communities, who have an extensive history of caring, are present everywhere, and mobilize extensive social capital.

That means that government and the public should encourage rather than discourage the large faith-based federations that are part of the disaster response system, such as Catholic Charities and the Salvation Army, to be robustly faithful in the assistance they offer. It also means that the disaster response system must reach out to equip and include churches and smaller parachurch ministries that comprise such an important part of the fabric of every community.

As David Mills, founder of *Family to Family* and the "Twin Towers Orphan Fund," writes,

The magnitude of faith community resources that can be applied to disaster relief and recovery can only be estimated by viewing the significance of other related faith-based involvement in charity. Faith-based charitable organizations hold five of the top ten national spots in charitable size, and churches are a primary source for all charitable volunteerism in both religious and secular charity. The Salvation Army raised more than any other national charity in 1997.

In virtually every city, town and rural area, faith-based providers already provide millions of tons of commodities to needy families and house tens of thousands of our homeless citizens. A 1993 study reported that the faith-based community provides more than 125 million hours per month of volunteer time to non-religious charitable activity.

The level of faith-based contribution is very substantial and includes: 87% of congregations reporting one or more programs related to human services, 60% reporting that their facilities were available to groups from the community, and 60% reporting that they provided in-kind support services like food and clothing. A report in the late 1980's identified more than 41 billion dollars per year being given by faith-based organizations to non-religious services. Faith-based organizations now command 34% of all volunteers and 10% of all wages and salaries in the non-profit sector. These facts clearly identify the faith-based community as a massive resource that is ready to respond to the critical needs raised by September 11th and the long-term needs to repair lives and communities that follow every disaster."[27]

THE UNITED WAY

In cities and larger towns, the United Way plays a key role in coordinating private social services and raising funds for them. Unfortunately, even though religious leaders pioneered the United Way concept more than a century ago in Denver, local United Way administrations have usually been skeptical about working with faith-based groups—except ones that didn't seem too sectarian. So even though churches and church-related programs are often the first place people turn to when they need help, church-related services usually have not been included in fundraising or in the planning and coordination of assistance.

Fortunately, some United Way leaders over the past few years have come to realize that it has been a mistake to leave churches and religious charities marginalized. One of the most striking fruits of this rethinking is the "Faith in Action Initiative" of the United Way of Massachusetts Bay, which serves Boston and the surrounding area. This initiative, which was begun in 1997, is devoted to nurturing and funding faith-based grassroots programs that serve at-risk young people.

Marian Heard, president and CEO of United Way of Massachusetts Bay, says, "Faith-based social ministries, while less visible than mainstream human services, are among groups which are often the most able to understand and respond to the needs of the communities in which they're based." When the organization decided to focus more on young people in poor neighborhoods, instead of just expanding its support to traditional service agencies, it decided to start the new initiative to build up the capacity of the faith-based groups that were already active and that touch young people's hearts.[28]

This is a notable reversal of the traditional United Way skittishness about faith. In fact, to win an award from the Faith in Action Initiative, the applicant group has to be able to demonstrate that faith is vital to the organization and its programs. Now that's a positive change of attitude!

LEARNING FROM 9/11

Remember those pastors who rushed to the Family Center to help the families of victims of the 9/11 terrorist attacks in New York City and were turned away because they were not part of the certified disaster response network? That shameful rejection of needed help has opened many eyes to the routine way in which abundant and essential resources of America's faith communities have been neglected by the coordinated disaster response system.

Yes, some faith-based organizations have long been active participants in our nation's disaster response and recovery efforts. Some of their names are familiar, like the Salvation Army and Catholic Charities. Others may be less well known, such as Church World Service, Operation Blessing, Convoy of Hope, Christian Reformed

World Relief Committee, Mennonite Disaster Services, and the North American Mission Board of the Southern Baptist Church.

Whether acclaimed or unacknowledged, the contributions of these organizations are significant. Yet their important work is only a part of the contribution that can be made by America's faith communities to the disaster response and recovery effort. How can these groups be more effectively and fully integrated in order to improve the response to emergencies and disasters?

- Churches and faith-based charities that already have some kind of tie to groups that are part of the response network need to be trained and mobilized.
- The vast and diverse array of congregations and grassroots religious groups that are not currently affiliated should be given an opportunity to be activated.
- Training materials and programs suited for faith-based volunteers and groups need to be created.
- A credentialing system needs to be developed that would allow volunteers and groups that are not active in the response system on a daily basis to be able to offer their help in time of crisis.
- A new National Faith-Based Emergency Response Council should be developed to plan and implement such efforts in conjunction with FEMA, the American Red Cross, the Salvation Army, and other organizations involved in the disaster response and relief system.

A CHALLENGE TO CHURCHES AND PARACHURCH MINISTRIES

Clearly, it is neither easy nor simple to improve the compassionate response of our society to those in our midst who have suffered from a disaster or who are daily confronted with poverty or social problems. Government rules that unjustly restrict the religious liberty of faith-based organizations need to be reformed. Professional training must become more respectful of faith commitments and the dynamic of faith in people's lives. Systems devised to coordinate disaster services need to open up to include neglected faith-community resources.

However, such changes will make little difference as long as evangelical Christians continue to hang back from full public engagement. As others are changing, will we change too? To be sure, it is safer to remain disengaged, to marginalize ourselves because we fear that collaborating with secular agencies and/or government programs will expose us to temptations and pressures or may even necessitate modifying or dropping religious emphases or activities that we have prized.

Yet if the mission of faith-based community service programs is to serve the community in the name of Christ, how can we refuse to be fully engaged? How can we relinquish opportunities to serve the community because we fear that we won't be able to testify to Christ? These are serious issues with which evangelicals must wrestle as we seek to be more fully obedient to Christ. After all, we are called not only to confess belief in him but also to follow him, and that includes serving our neighbors as effectively as possible. As we wrestle, we have much to learn from those Christian organizations that have lengthy experience operating in the public sphere and in partnering with government. We can observe compromises that were damaging and take note of dangers that must be more effectively avoided. We can also see a faithful witness to the gospel and to service in the name of Christ.

The Revolution of Compassion gives new opportunity for the Salvation Army, along with other faith-based organizations, to recover the possibility of providing social assistance in accord with its original vision. The future holds much promise for all of us, including the Army. As Charles Glenn writes, "The Salvation Army's ability to articulate a clear philosophy of service and its capacity for introspection and self-criticism are critical assets that have helped to safeguard its religious character to a large degree from both the internal and external pressures that are a reality for all faith-based organizations."[29]

The Revolution of Compassion has inspired a shift among many government employees, who in the past have viewed religious affiliation as irrelevant or problematic in providing social services. The work of the Salvation Army should be saluted for proving that faith does matter and that it is not an obstacle in delivering needed services. To the contrary, faith is the basis for every ministry's social

efforts, as the term *faith-based* implies. Moreover, faith-based organizations have demonstrated that they can partner with the government and with secular social agencies to achieve mutually acceptable
and desired social objectives.

William Booth offered a challenge that is still relevant to those
questioning the Salvation Army's commitment, effectiveness, and
passion for offering soup, soap, and salvation. It speaks to every
faith-based social service organization and to the government as
well: "All that I want is to have the work done. . . . If you have any
better plan than mine for effecting this purpose, in God's name
bring it to the light and get it carried out quickly. If you have not,
then lend me a hand with mine, as I would be only too glad to lend
you a hand with yours if it had in it greater promise of successful
action than mine."[30]

6

Equal Partners with Government

*Faith-based charities ought to be willing to engage the
state with the confidence that they are equal partners
in this enterprise, not just government contractors. . . .
Religious charities provide an immense help to the state
by providing social services in ways that the state itself
simply cannot provide. This should instill in the organizations that make up the religious social sector a deep
sense of the importance and uniqueness of their contribution to the general welfare. It should also strengthen their
determination, as they cooperate with various levels of
government in pursuit of common ends, to guard jeal-
ously their religious identity, knowing that it is precisely
because of it that they contribute to the public good.*

Luis Lugo, *Equal Partners:
The Welfare Responsibility
of Governments & Churches*

few months after George W. Bush became president and launched his initiative to elevate the role of "neighborhood healers," *New Yorker* magazine ran a cartoon showing a minister leading his congregation in supplicating God "to see to it that we get our hands on some of that government scratch."[1] Should your church or parachurch ministry pray for some of that "government scratch"? Or should you pray that the temptation will pass you by?

We have argued in this book that partnerships are a good thing—that when faith-based groups collaborate with government it benefits the groups and the government, and, most important, the people who need help. That's the general principle. However, not all partnerships are good. Government money brings burdens, such as paperwork, and it is accompanied by many rules. Although the faith-based movement is causing funding rules to be changed to become hospitable to churches and religious charities, many sources of government funding continue to have restrictive rules.

So in this chapter we will give you guidance about seeking government funding. What issues or concerns should you keep in mind when you consider the possibility of seeking government money to support your services? If you do accept government money, what action can you take to protect your ministry's mission? Equally important, when should you "just say 'no'" to government money? In this brief chapter we cannot cover all the details, and we specifically are not giving legal advice (for that you have to consult with an attorney), but we will lay out the big picture.

The First Rule for Seeking Government Funding Is: Don't Seek Government Funding First

Should your church go after government funding because Charitable Choice now tells officials they cannot arbitrarily exclude religious groups from competing for grants? Should your parachurch ministry start up an after-school program for kids at the struggling local public school because Congress has decided to

Help That's Helpless

The meetings of the Bethel Baptist Church's Mercy Committee typically run without a glitch—problems are raised, solutions are proposed, a vote is taken, a check is written, a program is launched, or some other decision is made. Today, however, a monkey wrench has been thrown into the engine of this well-oiled machine. A stranger has come to tonight's meeting with a proposal.

"Good evening, ladies and gentlemen, my name is Steve O'Neill. As an official from the Jackson County Welfare Department, I'm working with a family on welfare—a young single mother and her four kids. The mother really wants to get off welfare and become a self-sufficient, contributing member of society, but she hasn't managed to make it with the welfare checks and the training programs we have given her. Obviously, she needs our services, but her life just isn't pulled together. She feels hopeless about the future and is having trouble dealing with her kids and with her own depression. I think that you and the members of your church can offer the additional help she needs. I've heard that Bethel already helps people in its own congregation with financial seminars, parenting classes, and so on.

"So here's my proposal: I would like to match up this woman and her family with a support team from your church. My goal is for the team to help the family become independent of welfare within six months. My office would transfer to the church a year's worth of her welfare checks. Your team would control the money, work out a budget with the family, and help them to stick to it. The team would also pay for the mother to receive specialized training for a job that could support her family. The most important thing that Bethel can offer is a supportive network of people to offer advice to the family when they get in trouble and moral guidance to help them stay out of trouble.

"So what do you think? This family could really use your help. Will you join us in helping them out?"

The members of the committee look grave. Eyes dart around the room as they wait for someone to deliver what's on each of their minds. They begin to talk quietly among themselves. Finally, Mr. Winchell, the local pharmacist, speaks. "With all due respect, we at Bethel believe strongly that helping the poor is the task of the church and not the government's responsibility."

"Great!" exclaims Steve. "That means you'll help us out."

"Now hold on," rejoins Mr. Winchell. "Let me finish. That means that we prefer to help out those in need on our own terms, with our own money, and with our own way of doing things, which is to say, the Lord's way of doing things. It's not in keeping with our mission to mix our affairs with those of the government, if you know what I mean. We appreciate your offer, but I think I speak for the rest of the committee when I say, thanks, but no thanks. You'll have to help the family on your own. We don't want to get off our mission of helping the needy the right way."

fund such programs? Of course not! Just because money is available does not mean your group should go after it.

Long before searching for government funding, believers have other vital matters to consider. For example, just what are the pressing needs in the neighborhood and the wider community? Who is already working to meet those needs? Are those existing programs and groups doing effective work?

If effective programs already exist, then instead of trying to create another one, it might be better for people newly motivated to serve their neighbors to pour their energy, skills, and money into those good organizations. Instead of your church starting a new program, maybe it should channel volunteers and funds into that parachurch ministry or even into the programs operated by another church, a network of churches, an interfaith service group, or even a secular organization. The key is help that really helps, and not the growth and glory of the faith-based group.

On the other hand, maybe a new organization, or a new or expanded program of an existing group, really is needed. Still, the first issue cannot be how to get government funding for the new or expanded effort. Government money can be a wonderful resource that enables a faith-based group to expand the help it can offer, but it usually comes with many requirements and restrictions, and it may be available one year but not the next. Without care, the prospect of winning a large award can lead a group off mission, promising to do things that are not really close to its passion and calling.

So, before thinking about competing for government grants or contracts, a group should prayerfully and carefully decide just what is its passion and calling, come up with a plan for excellent service, and devise a sober budget. Then, instead of going right to government, search for long-term, committed support (not just money but prayer, volunteering, and advice) from people in the church and community. Make sure you know what you should be doing and how to do it and that you have a solid foundation of income and moral support from private sources. Then you'll be ready to consider whether government funding would be a help or a hindrance to your mission.

Finding Government Money

If government funding is appropriate, how can you find that government "scratch"? It turns out this is not such an easy task, but there are resources to help you.

The first thing is to ignore the persistent rumors. Despite all the stories, there is no pot of government money set aside for faith-based groups. That's right. There is no "faith-based money," no special federal fund of $20 million, or $4 billion, or $320 million set aside by the Bush administration specifically for churches and religious nonprofits. Nor should there be. It would not be right for officials to steer all funding to faith-based groups just because of their faith basis. What officials are supposed to do is to fund the groups that can provide the most effective help. They should not be biased against faith-based groups—that's why reforms are so important—but they should not be biased in favor of faith-based groups, either, as if all faith-based programs are good and all secular programs are bad.

So there's no pot of "faith-based money." Instead, there is a (somewhat) level playing field. Faith-based groups are not restricted to special faith-based funding but are eligible for *all* the money—not just a small part of it—that federal, state, and local governments spend to obtain welfare and social services for the needy. Remember from chapter 3 that a large majority of federal dollars for social programs is sent to state and local officials, who then usually award the money to outside agencies in the form of grants and contracts. State and local governments also fund a great many services on their own. In all the places where barriers have been removed, faith-based organizations are free to compete on equal terms with other groups to obtain a part of the government funds set aside for human services.

Government officials, however, make money available to support such services very differently than do private donors or foundations. With private money, usually the group seeking funding contacts individuals, companies, or foundations and asks them to help fund some service the group itself has designed. With government, things are normally the other way around. It is the government that first decides what kinds of services it will support and then advertises for private organizations that will provide those services with government help.

Government money is given out for specific services—money from a specific program run by a county department to assist the homeless, or money from the federal Department of Veterans Affairs to help homeless veterans, or money from a state human services department for assistance that will help poor families not become homeless. There is no money to support doing good in general but instead these are government programs for particular purposes, run by one or another federal, state, or local department.

A faith-based group looking for government support for its services for homeless families cannot just hunt around for an official with a heart for the poor, then present its story and hope to get government dollars. Instead, the group has to search for a match between the kinds of services it offers and the kinds of services that a federal, state, or local department is authorized to fund. That requires getting to know the government funding system, which is known as the grants system at the federal level and usually the procurement or contracting system at the state and local level. All these systems are the ways officials announce that funds are available, run competitions to see which applicants are best, award the funds, and monitor how the money is spent and whether the funded groups do any good.

What government money is available? Billions of dollars are given out annually, offered by specific programs within particular federal, state, and local departments. Groups looking for government support need to watch for announcements of funding availability, a request for proposals, a standard funding announcement, etc. The terms differ, but the idea is that at a particular time, maybe just once or twice a year, a government program announces that it is ready to accept applications from private groups that say they can provide the kind of services the government wants.

Sad to say, there is no single list of government grants or contracts, not even just for federal funds. On top of that, the grants and contracts process can be complicated, despite recent reforms. The various programs usually have somewhat different rules about what can and cannot be done. Application forms can be lengthy and complex, and the deadline for submitting applications might be only a month or two after the funding announcement. That is not much time to gather information about the organization and its experience, detail precisely the needs to be met, give the exact design of the service to be offered, and write a persuasive statement about why the service will be effective, how volunteers will be selected and trained, how funds will be allocated and accounted for, and more.

So, what to do? One thing is certain: a group interested in government funding should start right away to prepare by learning about the procurement process, finding out when and where grants and contracts are announced, and gaining skills in writing effective applications. That means looking for help!

Government departments themselves often can provide considerable information, listing on their websites current grant announcements, maintaining mailing lists of groups interested in finding out about new funding, printing brochures on how to apply for funds, and running bidders conferences to help potential applicants understand just what the department is seeking. Larger communities sometimes have nonprofit resource centers, and some colleges or community colleges offer courses on searching for grants and writing grant applications. Of course, a great place to turn for advice is to another faith-based organization that already has experience obtaining and managing government money.

Check to see if your denomination provides guidance and information. For example, the Church of the Nazarene's Compassionate Ministries pays particular attention to the faith-based initiative (http://www.nazarenecompassion.org), and the United Methodist Church has published guidelines for member churches concerning government funding—"Community Ministries and Government Funding" (http://www.umc.org). Dr. Bob Reccord, president of the Southern Baptist North American Mission Board, says, "We will seek primarily to become a resource to churches across the SBC in knowing how to deal with government agencies and of what parameters they should be cautious." He adds, "We will also coordinate with such organizations as We Care America and the Southern Baptist Ethics and Religious Liberty Commission to offer the best advice and resources possible in this area."[2]

Many communities also have one or more networks of service providers (faith-based, secular, or mixed) with a small staff that is knowledgeable about government as well as private funding sources. Remember, too, one of the great innovations of the movement to expand partnerships: faith and community liaisons—those government officials or offices designated to help faith-based and grassroots groups understand and navigate relations with government. There is also an increasing number of groups formed specifically to help faith-based groups think through government funding and go after the funds if appropriate.

Finding Help in Locating and Applying for Government Funding

GOVERNMENT RESOURCES

- White House Office of Faith-Based and Community Initiatives: http://www.fbci.gov
- Centers for Faith-Based and Community Initiatives: go to http://www.fbci.gov and follow the links to the various Centers for Faith-Based and Community Initiatives
- State, regional, and local faith and community liaisons: for a list go to the Charitable Choice area of http://www.cpjustice.org

FAITH COMMUNITY RESOURCES

- We Care America: http://www.wecareamerica.org
- Faith in Communities Initiative at the Hudson Institute: http://www.hudsonfaithincommunities.org

DOS AND DON'TS OF GOVERNMENT FUNDING

Should your church or parachurch ministry go after government dollars? A faith-based organization that says *yes* to government funds "increases greatly the number of persons it can help and thereby expands the needs it is meeting, the good it is doing, and the influence it is exerting," as Stephen Monsma says. Yet he emphasizes that there is a condition attached to that good outcome. The faith-based group has to proceed "with its eyes wide open, realizing the dangers that can arise in accepting government money." It also needs to have "a self-conscious strategy for avoiding these dangers."[3]

The dangers do not mean faith-based groups must stay as far away from government as possible; if things were that bad, we would not recommend that you consider partnerships, of course. Yet Monsma is right: groups need a deliberate strategy to counteract the potential problems. As the Boy Scouts say: "Be Prepared!"

The biggest threat, as evangelical groups know, is that the rules that government sometimes attaches to its funds will damage the faith character of an organization and that by accepting government money, an organization will lose its autonomy and become prey to even greater restrictions in the future. There are other dangers, too, such as getting into legal trouble for not carefully accounting for how government funds were spent.

We have chosen some of the key challenges that face faith-based organizations that accept government money and offer ten guidelines to help keep the groups on the right track.

1. Know Your Mission

The single most important thing for a faith-based organization to do when it considers seeking government money is to make sure it knows what its mission is. In the words of a guide for United Methodist churches, "No religious organization should embark on the course of becoming a faith-based provider of government-funded social services before deciding that it fits the organization's *religious* mission." It would be foolish to take on the paperwork and regulations that come with government money "without first determining what services, precisely, the church is *called* to supply to the community."[4]

Without clarity about mission, how can a group avoid chasing after funds and promising that it will supply whatever services government officials (or foundations or corporate donors) are willing to pay for, even though the group is not prepared to provide those services with excellence, and even though the whole purpose of the group was originally something else? Without clarity about mission, how can a faith-based organization shape services, its management style, and its employment rules to reflect the religious vision it professes? If it cannot do that, then it will be different from secular groups only in intention or inspiration, not in the way needs are understood and assistance offered.

Amy Sherman said it well: "First, clearly discern and articulate your mission and pursue it faithfully—with or without government funding. The availability of new funding sources should not drive your ministry's outreach endeavors. Rather, you must know what you are called to do and then assess whether a relationship with government will complement or facilitate your community work."[5]

A brief word about a sensitive subject: evangelization. If evangelization is your group's burning mission, then you should not be looking to government for your funding. Faith-based organizations that offer government-funded services are free to share the gospel in many ways, and they should, but the government money is intended for "this-worldly" help (to use Stephen Monsma's useful term). The money cannot be diverted to buying tracts, enlarging the church, or paying the minister's salary. Nor is it honest for a group to assume the responsibility of teaching job skills or taking care of children if it intends to preach the Good News rather than provide excellent training and care. Seeing clients only as a mission field may devalue them. Many of them may be unsaved, but others are believers who have been brought down due to the mistakes or sins of others. Even unsaved clients have arrived with some other need—the problem that brought them to the program in the first place. A faith-based group that advertises that it will tend to this-worldly needs certainly should do no less than tend excellently to those needs.

For guidance on the liberties of and restrictions on faith-based organizations that accept federal and other government funds, see:

- White House Office of Faith-Based and Community Initiatives, "Guidance to Faith-Based and Community Organizations on Partnering with the Federal Government" (December 2002).
- Amy Sherman, *The Charitable Choice Handbook for Ministry Leaders* (Washington, D.C.: Center for Public Justice, 2001).

2. Don't Hide Your Light under a Bushel

Clarity about mission is important not only internally but also externally. People searching for help need to know whether a group is really faith-based or if it just has some historic religious connection. Then people who for whatever reason object to religion or to a particular faith can look for a different provider, and the many who prefer to be helped by programs that take faith seriously know where to turn for assistance.

Government officials also need to know about their organizational partners. Equal treatment requires officials to acknowledge particular duties and freedoms for faith-based providers, such as their liberty under many laws to take faith into account in employment decisions. Because church-state issues are complicated, it is important for faith leaders and government officials to talk through matters such as how to respond to the person who seeks spiritual counsel in the middle of a budgeting class or the other person who might be better helped by a secular program that has different strengths.

It can be tempting for a group to downplay its faith character if the officials in charge of awarding contracts are prejudiced against faith-based providers. A better solution is to appeal to their supervisors or to have your lawyer have a heart-to-heart talk with the officials or their supervisors. Or maybe your group, or a coalition of faith-based groups, should lobby the governor or mayor to ask for fair treatment and religious liberty. Pretending to be something you are not may work in the short term, but it does not establish a good foundation for a long-term relationship, and it allows officials to continue to abuse their office by discriminating against faith.

Amy Sherman prepared an excellent tool for faith-based groups called a "Code of Conduct." She says it is "a way for faith-based groups to communicate to government, the public, clients, and faith communities how they will conduct themselves when they accept government funds." It is a way to tell officials (and also supporters) that your organization is committed in principle—and not just by government requirement—to effective help, respectful treatment of the religious convictions of clients, and careful handling of funds. The "Code of Conduct" is reprinted at the back of this book. Study it, copy it, sign it, and use it when you talk with officials about grants and contracts.

3. Don't Get Hooked on Government Money

If 100 percent of your group's funding comes from government, how likely is it that you will say *no* when a government official imposes some new religious restriction? Even if the proportion from government (or from a foundation or a large donor) is half or two-thirds, the group is faced with a tough choice: give in to an unwise or even sinful demand or close down a large part of its operations. The old saying really is true: whoever pays the piper calls the tune. If most of the money comes from the government, officials will feel justified in dominating the relationship, and the ministry's leaders will have little bargaining power to resist.[6]

So to retain autonomy, faith-based organizations should limit how much money they accept from government (or any other single source). In other words, groups should be sure their funding comes from multiple sources. What is the tolerable upper limit for government dollars? There is no firm rule, but it stands to reason that a group is not really very independent if it gets half or more of its income from government.

Keeping the percentage down is only one essential step however. The other is to plan ahead how to handle pressures. Just which restrictions on religious activities are appropriate and which must be resisted? The staff and governing board of each group that accepts government money "must draw its own line beyond which it will not go."[7] The leadership has to plan ahead about how it will either replace the rejected government funds or shrink its programs without harming the people it has chosen to serve.

Besides taking steps to maintain its *independence* from government, a faith-based organization should also work hard to maintain its *dependence* on its community of believers. Without care, a group can devote so much attention to getting and managing government money that it neglects to cultivate the supporters who believe heart and soul in its whole mission. Yet these supporters are a source of the other income that enables the group to maintain independence from government. They are also the ministry's prayer warriors. They will be the ones, not government officials, who warn when compromises are looming and who recall why the ministry was started in the first place.

Faithful supporters do not have to be lost when a ministry brings in government funds. Recall in the survey at the end of chapter 3 that 90 percent of the faith-based groups reported that this was not a problem for them. Yet it is a real danger. To prevent it, keep reporting back to supporters and not just to the government's contract monitors.

4. Red Tape Isn't All Bad

This is not a secret: government money always comes with a lot of rules and requires a lot of paperwork. There may be too much paperwork, and some of the rules are excessive or wrong, but the underlying principle is right: organizations entrusted with government money and with the task of assisting vulnerable people have to be accountable for how they use the money and how they carry out the task. Yes, of course, churches and parachurch ministries are first and foremost accountable to God, but they are also accountable to others, including the government.[8]

People who believe in the Bible should be keenly aware of how easy it is for well-intentioned people to do the wrong thing and how much we all need to give an accounting for our actions to others. So bemoan the excesses of government regulation and cheer on the reformers who are working to cut red tape. At the same time, however, use the rules and paperwork as tools to help you be a good steward, making sure money is accounted for precisely and used wisely, staff and volunteers follow the rules, and the services offered make a measurable difference for the people who have turned to your program for help.

Think the red tape is just too much? Here's great advice: "Keep your eyes on the prize: service to those in need. If good and valuable services can be provided only through contracts entailing mountains of paperwork, grit your teeth and climb the mountain."[9]

5. Strength in Numbers

Are the government grants or contracts always so large they would swamp your organization's budget? Would it be foolish to promise to help as many students or trainees as the officials desire? Does the government have accounting and reporting requirements that go beyond what your group is able to handle? Then do not seek funding on your own, but join with other groups.

Here is how to accept the government money without losing your shirt:

- Become a subcontractor to an experienced larger group. They will have most of the managerial and accounting burden; you will only be responsible for as much service as you can handle, and you will have a chance to learn from others.
- Join with other churches to establish a new nonprofit organization that can manage government awards and coordinate the services offered by each of the affiliated congregations.

- Contract with a larger organization to be the award administrator, freeing your group to concentrate on providing help instead of managing money.

Partnerships like these are great ways to spread information and skills and to ensure that smaller groups do not get in over their heads. They are also a great way to knit together large religiously affiliated organizations—organizations that have great expertise but may have lost their roots in congregations—with fresh new groups, enthusiastic about service but lacking experience. Go talk with your local branch of the Salvation Army, Lutheran Services of America, or Catholic Charities.

6. Protect Your Church by Creating a Separate Nonprofit for Social Service

Churches that decide to seek government funding should establish a separate nonprofit organization to accept the government money and operate the social services. Nonprofit incorporation is done through a designated agency in each state, which enforces requirements such as having a governing board and bylaws and devoting all income to services rather than profit. Groups also often apply to the Internal Revenue Service for 501(c)(3) tax status, exempting them from federal and state corporate income taxes.

Why bother with the time and expense for all this?[10] One benefit is making sure that all the government money goes to providing social services and is not inadvertently used for church expenses. Also, if the government requires or conducts an audit of the grant or contract funds, the examination will be restricted to the separate nonprofit and not result in anyone roaming through the church's books and policies. (Some versions of Charitable Choice allow government funds to be put into a separate account and limit government audits to that separate account.) Equally important, having a separate structure shields the church from various civil rights requirements that accompany government money.

Having IRS 501(c)(3) status may encourage greater private giving because donors can deduct their contributions from their federal taxes (if they itemize). Sometimes foundations or corporations require groups to have 501(c)(3) status to be eligible for their grants.

There are other benefits of a separate organization, too. Meeting the requirements for nonprofit incorporation can strengthen a ministry because the process requires clarity about mission, naming a governing board, and creating a management structure. Dedicating a structure separate from the church focuses its staff, volunteers, board, and supporters on its own particular mission of social services—services that are faith-based but distinct from worship and evangelism.

7. Become Friends with a Lawyer

Whenever a lot of legal details are involved, a wise person consults with a legal expert. That precaution surely applies in the case of a faith-based organization accepting government money. By taking the money, you are accepting the responsibility to abide by the rules and reporting requirements, and there are consequences for falling short. Your organization might have to return unspent funds, return all funds, pay a fine, or suffer some other penalty if you break any of the rules. So when you look at the details of a government grant or contract, and certainly when it comes time to sign the paperwork for the money, you need to have an experienced and faith-friendly lawyer looking over your shoulder and advising you about the fine print and the legal obligations. You will want a lawyer to work with you, too, when you seek nonprofit incorporation and apply for IRS 501(c)(3) status.

Just as important, you will need to call on a lawyer if you run into a government official who does not know—or refuses to acknowledge—that changes like Charitable Choice require fair treatment in place of the traditional bias against groups considered "too religious." A call or visit from a lawyer to remind the official what the law and Constitution require may be all that is necessary to remove the obstacle to fair treatment.

Not all lawyers specialize in nonprofit and religious liberties issues. Check the resources section at the end of the book for some recommendations about how to find the right one.

8. Advocacy Is a Way to Serve

Often our neighbors in distress need a "cup of cold water"—a bag of groceries, subsidized child care, or some other service. Sometimes, however, they need a defender and advocate—someone who will challenge the powerful on their behalf.

- Instead of a welfare check, a mother needs someone to help her persuade an official to make her children's father pay the child support he owes.
- The mom needs the welfare check but cannot get it unless someone will intervene to persuade the caseworker to overturn an erroneous decision to deny benefits.
- Mom and Dad are determined to support the family by starting a small business, but they cannot do it until the city council overturns complex and expensive requirements that hobble entrepreneurial small businesses such as nail care and hair braiding salons.
- The family is doing its best, but its progress is undermined because the police do not aggressively challenge drug dealers, the public transportation system does not connect the inner city with the suburbs where the new jobs are being created, and, despite periodic promises, the neighborhood public schools are neither safe nor effective at teaching.

In situations like these, charity is no substitute for justice, and service is no substitute for advocacy and action. So this is just a reminder that faith-based organizations that collaborate with government have to retain their autonomy so they can challenge officials when needed. Silence in the face of injustice should never be the price of government funding.

9. Cultivate Champions

Good works are more persuasive than arguments. So one of the best ways to protect faith-based programs from attacks and excessive restrictions is to let people see the actual good they do. After all, many politicians and reporters who worry that government partnerships with faith-based programs will fatally undermine the Constitution are sympathetic toward groups that actually serve the downtrodden and are intrigued about programs that really do liberate the addicted. Seeing how good programs operate is the best antidote for the critics' fears that church-related programs are only interested in forcing religion on unwilling clients.

So make influential people your allies by letting them see what your faith-based organization does. Faith-based groups, Stephen Monsma recommends, should "cultivate and maintain good relationships with the media and elected officials."[11] Invite reporters to talk with people your programs have helped. Get to know your elected representatives, introduce them to your group, and have them speak at the annual banquet or march with you when your group parades to take back the neighborhood from gangs and drug dealers.

Then, if radical church-state separationists or a government official tries to stir up opposition, your group will be able to draw on "a reservoir of goodwill and sympathetic understanding." Critics with an axe to grind and obstructionist officials will not make much headway if an elected representative is a champion of the program. The law may not safeguard faith-based charities as well as it should, Monsma points out, "but the potential political and public relations protections are strong."[12]

10. Stand Up and Push Back!

"Pre-emptive capitulation." That's the provocative phrase Luis Lugo uses to describe what too many Christian organizations do when they fear that officials or the public will judge their programs to be too religious. We stifle ourselves, muffling or eliminating an activity that we think is essential and legal but that offends the politically correct. Or, faced with a contract that seems too restrictive but which the official on the other side of the desk claims is the way things have to be, we cave in, replaying in our heads those stories about faith-based groups harassed by extreme church-state separationists and forgetting about Charitable Choice and other liberating court rulings and legal changes.[13]

Let's be clear: There are plenty of aggressive and well-financed opponents of Christian ministry. Many officials are part of the Revolution of Compassion, but others are bitter opponents. Some laws have been made faith-friendly, but others are highly restrictive. Some elected officials' warm support of the faith-based initiative is revealed to be only lip service when the gay lobby, public-sector unions, or church-state separationists threaten opposition at the polls.

It would be foolish to pretend that the whole world and government have all of a sudden become the best friends of church-based social programs. Instead, faith-based groups need to proceed with care as they venture into the public square. Be sure that the way you treat clients and handle government money cannot be faulted by any fair observer. Ensure that your services are effective and powerful. Fulfill the promises you made when you signed the contract or grant.

Having made sure that your programs and practices are above reproach, be bold! Stand up to carping critics who have nothing real to object to but are just nostalgic for the old secularist days. Don't just slink away if an official says your group is "too religious" to be considered for funding. Don't just stop some religious activity because a reporter or official grimaces. Know what is permitted and how the courts and policymakers are becoming ever more favorable to the transformative power of faith in social services.

Now is the time to stand up and push back! Government and the public are looking for real answers, for programs that work. If we've got them, how can we just hide?

GOVERNMENT IS GOD'S SERVANT FOR GOOD

Secularizing pressures, outright discrimination, and petty requirements make it all too easy for evangelicals to slip into thinking of government as the enemy and government officials as necessarily out to hobble Christian ministries, but that kind of sweeping negative generalization conflicts with the Bible. The Apostle Paul states plainly in Romans 13 that government is established by God for good and is due our respect and honor (and taxes). Government funds expand a ministry's ability to serve and increase its influence, and government's accountability requirements can help ministries use resources wisely and effectively.

Beyond that, of course, many government officials are believers—fellow Christians. Administering a government program, monitoring the use of funds, developing welfare policy, or cracking down on contract fraud is their calling, their way of honoring God while showing love of neighbor. Such officials welcome the

Revolution of Compassion and await with us the day when excessive restrictions, poorly designed programs, and mountains of paperwork will be gone.

Instead of suspicion, ministries would do better to adopt an attitude of "discerning teachableness" toward government officials. The term is from Amy Sherman, who says, be careful as you collaborate with government officials so you can discern where "secular values and philosophies" may distort their views, but don't stop there. "Many governmental bureaucrats have good counsel and practical wisdom to offer Christians desiring to begin or enhance community outreach."[14] They often know about a neighborhood's needs and the other organizations serving there, they can teach how to work cross-culturally, and they can provide training in grant writing and help in structuring an organization to be effective and efficient.

WHAT IF THE MONEY IS NOT COVERED BY CHARITABLE CHOICE?

Charitable Choice is a powerful symbol and example of the Revolution of Compassion. It is an outstanding reform that changes the rules of federal government funding so that previously marginalized faith-based groups can join in partnership. However, the new liberating rules apply only to a few programs—to state, local, and federal programs that use federal welfare, community-services, and drug treatment funds. So if Charitable Choice is so good, isn't it pointless for church and parachurch leaders to even consider all the federal, state, and local money that is not covered by it?

That is a hasty and wrong conclusion. Government funding of religious organizations did not start with Charitable Choice. We saw in chapter 2 that, before Charitable Choice, many religious groups that received government funds to serve children and families were in every way faith-based. Those groups were often under much pressure to minimize their faith character, but we should not over-emphasize the problem. Organizations like the Salvation Army have wrestled with the pressures without giving up. Besides, President Bush's equal treatment executive order, which he signed in December 2002 (see chapter 3), tells federal, state, and local officials who spend federal funds that they cannot be biased against faith-based service groups.

What Charitable Choice does is *clarify* and *standardize*. It makes it clear that officials must follow the "equal treatment" guideline instead of the old no-aid discrimination. It also establishes a solid set of standards for officials and faith-based organizations, in place of the previous inconsistent rules and practices.

These are wonderful advances! You should not assume, however, that if Charitable Choice is absent, then officials will certainly discriminate against faith-based groups or must hand you a contract that demands hiding all religious symbols and ignoring the faith beliefs of job applicants. The regulations for some federal, state, and local government programs really are very restrictive, but other programs do not have restrictive regulations. Often when officials have resisted working with faith-based groups, it was because they believed that is what the Constitution required—overlooking the fact that the courts have shifted their interpretation from "no-aid" to "equal treatment."

So if there is no Charitable Choice, do not give up. Instead, look carefully at the funding announcement and the program rules to see whether there actually are unacceptable restrictions on participation. If you can, find a faith-based provider that has received or explored funding from this program and ask them about restrictions and how to cope with them. If the rules do not bar faith-based groups but the officials in charge are obstinate, you may have to appeal to a supervisor or an elected official, or get your lawyer involved. Of course, if you decide to sign a contract or grant, be sure to have the lawyer review the terms and conditions.

What If the Money Is Covered by Charitable Choice but Officials Are Resistant?

Sad to say, even if Charitable Choice does cover the funds, you won't always find smooth sailing. Recall the discussion about incomplete compliance in chapter 3. Faith-based groups are sometimes still excluded or discover when it is time to sign the paperwork that officials are demanding a restriction that Charitable Choice does not permit. The officials might simply be ignorant, or their hands might be tied because the governor or the head of the welfare department prefers the old status quo in place of Charitable Choice.

Whatever the reason, this is the time to be assertive (unless you have a good reason to keep quiet, such as the greater value of building a long-term relationship with the official and department). You and your lawyer, and maybe some fellow faith leaders, should have a serious talk with the recalcitrant official. You are in the right and the official is in the wrong, so a vigorous discussion may persuade the official to back down and comply with Charitable Choice or set in motion a rethinking by the department about its lack of compliance. (To equip you and your lawyer, the Center for Public Justice publishes a *Guide to Charitable Choice,* which includes the actual 1996 Charitable Choice language, and *Charitable Choice for Welfare & Community Services: An Implementation Guide for State, Local, and Federal Officials,* which includes the 1996 and 1998 Charitable Choice language and a detailed checklist to help officials come into compliance. See the resources section for these and other tools.)

FAITH-SENSITIVE STAFFING

Choosing only believers for a faith-based organization's staff can be a contentious and confusing issue. Many faith-based groups insist they must be able to hire on a religious basis or else they will soon no longer be faith-based. This is a make-or-break issue for them when they think about government money. (Not all faith-based groups agree: some are only concerned about the religion of the top leaders, others just want to be sure that no employee actively opposes the group's religious standards, and some make it a point to have a multi-faith staff because their clients have many different faiths.)

Many of the bitterest opponents of the faith-based initiative, however, have the exact opposite view. Religious staffing is rank discrimination, they claim, and if a faith-based group practices job discrimination with government money, then its action is not only morally wrong but illegal and unconstitutional. The rule, they say, is that any group that takes federal dollars agrees to hire without regard to faith, just as it must hire without regard to race, color, national origin, gender, age, or disability (there is no general federal employment rule about homosexuals).

So they say—but the statement is wrong. There is no general federal rule requiring all groups that accept government money to ignore religion in their employment decisions. There is a general federal rule about religious staffing, but it does not specifically mention government funds. The general rule is that faith-based organizations have the liberty to staff on a religious basis. That liberty is incorporated into the fundamental federal law on employment: the 1964 Civil Rights Act, as amended in 1972. (The law only applies to organizations with fifteen or more full-time employees; smaller organizations are not subject to this law at all.) A religious organization is free to require that its staff be believers who are committed to the organization's religious vision and standards. Like other organizations, though, the faith-based institution cannot discriminate on the grounds of race, color, national origin, and so on.

This liberty is not a violation of federal law or an exemption from it, as opponents and reporters commonly say. No, the liberty is built into the law. Secular groups cannot discriminate on a religious basis, because religion is irrelevant to their organization. Religious organizations, however, can take religion into account: after all, religion is what defines them. The liberty is not narrow. It applies to all religious organizations, not just churches and seminaries, and to all job positions, not just executives and chaplains but also receptionists and janitors. That is what the federal law says, and when the law was challenged by critics who claimed that, surely, a faith-based organization cannot fire a "secular" employee on religious grounds, the U.S. Supreme Court unanimously said that the law and Constitution certainly gave the faith-based organization exactly that liberty (*Corporation of the Presiding Bishop v. Amos,* 1987—a case about a janitor in a Mormon health club).[15]

States, and usually larger municipalities also, often have their own employment or human rights codes, which may be more restrictive than the federal law—for example, governing smaller organizations or adding additional protected categories, such as forbidding discrimination against homosexuals. Most of the time, however, these laws also include an exemption for faith-based organizations.

So those are the general rules—the rules that apply just because a faith-based organization gets started and hires people. What about religious staffing if a faith-based group decides to accept government money? Are the critics right that when government money enters, the religious staffing liberty departs?

The critics are wrong; the religious staffing liberty does not automatically depart when a faith-based organization accepts government money. Beyond that statement, however, there is no general rule but rather a variety of circumstances. Here is certainly an area where a faith-based organization needs to be guided by a good legal advisor. The following information is no substitute for discussing employment rules with a lawyer.

In brief, here are the different situations:

Direct Grants from the Federal Government

- Many direct federal grants are silent about employment. Faith-based groups are free to hire and fire on a religious basis.
- Other direct federal grants require all awardees to agree not to discriminate in hiring on a range of bases, including religion. Here faith-sensitive staffing is out, until the law is changed or the requirement is declared unconstitutional or illegal.

Funds Covered by Charitable Choice

- When federal, state, or local governments use federal welfare, Community Services Block Grant, or drug treatment funds, faith-based contractors and grantees may take faith into account in staffing. Because this interpretation of Charitable Choice is disputed by some and this liberty may conflict with a state or local government's usual practice, you may need to consult with a lawyer and exert pressure to get the liberty acknowledged.

State or Local Government Grants and Contracts

- When state or local governments use their own funds (or federal funds where religious staffing is not protected), they can require all recipients to agree not to use religion as a criterion for employment.

- State and local grants or contracts do not always forbid religious staffing. Even where they do, a faith-based organization may be able to successfully challenge the restriction on religious liberty on constitutional grounds.

(Note that by executive order in December 2002 President Bush amended a previous federal requirement about contractors with the federal government so that religious organizations that staff on a religious basis now may contract to provide goods and services to the federal government. Such contracts are distinct from federal grants to organizations to provide social services to people in need and are distinct from state and local contracts to provide social services to people in need.)

So religious staffing by faith-based organizations that accept government money is neither forbidden nor permitted across the board. Groups have to examine the rules that apply to any particular funding program in which they are interested.

By the way, faith-based groups would be wise to adopt a specific policy on religious staffing. Otherwise it may look to potential employees, the public, and the courts to be a mere convenient prejudice when a particular applicant is rejected or a staffer is fired with the claim that he or she does not meet a religious standard. Clarity about standards is equally important whether or not the religious organization accepts government money.

BROWNIES AND SALADS: WHEN FAITH IS BUILT INTO SOCIAL SERVICE

Believers, not the government, should fund worship and evangelism. Good enough. Yet what about a faith-based program, say one that works with drug addicts, alcoholics, or the long-term homeless, in which religious activities are part and parcel of the social service itself? What if giving their hearts to Jesus is the way certain people stop giving their lives to alcohol or drugs? In that case, if the government funds the program, is it funding religion—which it shouldn't—or an effective social service—which it should?

Sad to say, the courts have not progressed as far as they should in this matter, and therefore the law is not as liberating as it ought to be. You might think that, as long as people have a choice about where they can go for help, then it should not be a problem if the government funds a program in which a person escapes addiction and becomes a good citizen, employee, and family member through religious transformation. Of course, such a transformation is good, but for now, the government cannot give grants or contracts to programs that depend on religious activities such as evangelism, worship, or discipleship as the form of assistance. (Such programs can get government money through indirect funding, though. See the next section of this chapter.)

Is that restriction wrong? Isn't the faith-based initiative intended to eliminate such discrimination, to create a truly level playing field on which all service programs can compete? All true. However, until the courts move even further away from the "no-aid" idea and even more firmly adopt the "equal treatment" interpretation, government officials, including legislators devising reforms like Charitable Choice, are restricted in what they can do. For now, the courts' commitment to equal treatment is undercut by a concern that if an official awards a grant or a contract to a program that includes religious activities, it will appear that the government is unconstitutionally endorsing those activities and that religion. That is unfortunate and unfair, but it is the reality.

Let's not forget, however, that by design, many faith-based programs do not use discipleship training and worship as their chief means of providing help. They offer job training and life-skills courses in a loving and respectful environment, and they also invite those they help to worship on Sunday, to join a Bible study, or to seek pastoral counseling. They witness to the Good News in every way but do not think that helping a person prepare for the GED is the same as teaching them the Gospel of John. They offer a warm bed and a warm meal and also the Good News, but they are convinced that no one should be required to listen to the Bible in order to get a meal or a safe place to sleep.

Amy Sherman calls the two different kinds of ministries "salad ministries" and "brownie ministries."[16] What's the difference? "Salad ministries" have programs with various parts, some that are clearly religious and some that are not, just as a salad is a combination of tomatoes, lettuce, and other ingredients. These ministries offer both Bible-based life-skills training and Microsoft-based job training on word processing and spreadsheets. The government funds the job training, and the church funds the life-skills class. Everyone is invited to both, but no one has to listen to the pastor talk about biblical principles for life if they have decided they only want to learn how to use the computer. (They might already be learning life skills from someone in their own church.)

"Brownie ministries" do not have the same kind of separation between program elements. Like a brownie, the ingredients are all blended and baked together. The alcoholic gets medical help that is connected with spiritual counseling, which flows into intensive and constant worship and Bible study, and these undergird close mentoring relationships. For this kind of ministry, salvation from alcoholism is a side effect of a commitment to Jesus Christ. Religious activities and religious change are the social service.

It is not appropriate to ask which kind of ministry is better than the other. What style of ministry is better depends on the kind of need, who is helping, and who is coming for help. Working through such issues is absolutely essential for every ministry.

One thing is very clear, however. "Brownie" ministries should not try to pretend they are "salad" ministries in order to obtain grants or contracts. What gain would there be in destroying the ministry in order to expand it? "Salad" ministries can accept grants or contracts in good conscience because they separate inherently religious elements from the other parts of their assistance out of conviction, not because of government pressure. For them the challenge is to maintain a strong conception of "holism"—that both kinds of assistance are vital even though, out of respect, no one will be forced to participate in discipleship or worship activities. Without care, the two dimensions of service will fall apart rather than support each other.

Interview on 25 November 2002 with Wade Horn, assistant secretary for the Administration for Children and Families, Department of Health and Human Services

---

Q: Some faith-based organizations object to the government's requirement that religious activities like evangelism and worship have to be voluntary for clients and cannot be paid for with government funds. What do you say to them?

A: It is true that there are limits to what you can do with government money if you're a faith-based organization. Because of these limitations, some faith-based organizations may come to the conclusion, "Well, I don't want to do that! I think a big part of the success of my program is the fact that I bring this person to faith. It is not just a social service we provide. Bringing a person to faith is indispensable to what we do. I'm not willing to stop doing that in order to get federal funds."

So that group may reject the idea of applying for federal funding. I think that may be a reasonable decision for such an organization to make. As government officials, we have a responsibility to describe clearly what the legal limitations connected with federal grants are, so that faith-based organizations can make good decisions based on whether or not the limitations are acceptable to them.

Q: But what if a group is convinced of the importance of evangelism and wants to share the faith with everyone? Do they have to get rid of all faith from their program?

A: Not at all. For example, a church could use federal welfare money, received through state or local officials, to set up in their church basement a training facility to give computer training to welfare recipients. In doing so, that church wouldn't have to take down the crosses or other religious icons on the wall. While their clients are in that government-funded program, the church couldn't spend time evangelizing them. But that doesn't mean the church couldn't hold a worship service on Sunday or a Bible study in the evening and let the people in the computer class know they are welcome to join them on Sunday or in the evening. What that church couldn't do is tell them, "If you want to continue in this training program, you have to come to our Bible study." The church can let them know about the Bible study but it has to be their choice whether or not to attend.

There's a fine line here between what is appropriate and what is not. Some programs do things inadvertently that can get them in trouble. For example, an adult literacy program might be tempted to use the Bible as its textbook. You can't do that. Or an abstinence program might be tempted to teach the story of the virgin birth as an example of staying abstinent until you are married. You can't do that either.

I don't think faith-based programs are trying to be cute and ignore appropriate limits. It's just that the Bible and their faith is so central to their being, they just naturally come up with the Bible as a text or the virgin birth as their key example. I don't think they are trying to skirt the law. I just think it's part of their being. So we have to be clear what the limits are.

Q: I've heard that the rules are not as restrictive in the case of indirect
government funding such as vouchers. Can you explain that?

A: With indirect funding, the government funding goes out in the form of a
voucher given to a recipient, instead of in the form of a government grant or
contract given directly to the service provider. Then the recipient gives the
voucher to the provider and receives the service, and the provider turns over the
vouchers to the government and gets payment for the services it has provided.

What's important is that when the money goes out in the form of
a voucher to an individual who then uses it to obtain services, and the
individual has a choice of various providers, then it is the individual who
decides what group will provide the service and then get the government
funding. As the Supreme Court recently confirmed again, in such a case of
choice, the voucher is considered to be assistance to the individual, not to
the organization. And the courts say a faith-based organization that gets
funded through these vouchers isn't under the same limitations on religious
activities as a group that gets government funds directly by a grant or
contract. With vouchers, those limits on religious expression and activities
aren't applied to the faith-based organization. That's important for groups
that consider Bible study or conversion essential to their program of service.

I happen to run perhaps the largest voucher program in America. It's
called "child care." Each year the federal government gives $4.8 billion to
the states in the form of block grants. And the states must give the parents
a choice about where they will get their child care. They have to offer the
choice of a referral to a child-care provider who has a contract with the state
or else a voucher that the parents can take to a provider of their own choice.
Eighty-three percent of all the child-care money that currently goes to the
states actually is distributed in the form of vouchers given to parents. Only
17 percent is spent in contracting with child-care providers.

Why is this important? Well, parents who get a child-care voucher can
take it to a child-care program run by a church, synagogue, or mosque. And
those houses of worship don't have to secularize their programs in any way.
So you can still pray, you can still talk about the faith—you can do those
things that are not allowed when the funding is by direct grant or contract to
the faith-based provider itself.

So, if your faith-based organization operates a child-care facility, guess
what? It is probably eligible to accept vouchers from parents. If it meets
the registration or licensing requirements of the state agency that runs the
subsidized child-care system, then it can provide government-funded care
without religious limitations, as long as it follows other requirements such
as health and safety rules. It doesn't have to limit faith the way it would if it
accepted a grant or contract directly from the government.

GOVERNMENT MONEY FOR "BROWNIE" PROGRAMS

Do those restrictions on grants and contracts seem too confining? It so happens that there is a different way government can fund faith-based programs, which does not require them to separate the inherently religious activities out from the rest of the assistance they offer. It's called "indirect" funding.

Here's the basic idea: if the person needing help, instead of a government official, decides the government money should go to a faith-based group, then no one can think the government is singling out that group for favor. So then it does not matter if that group's programs have religious activities built into them; even if government money supports those programs, there's no violation of the ban on government establishing religion. With indirect funding, "brownie" programs that include discipleship training as an integral part of the service can be funded by government.

Of course, the purpose of the government funding is still to help the person get off drugs, into work, or out of a life of crime. The programs that government funds indirectly still have to have such purposes and effects. The money cannot be used merely for evangelism with the argument that saved people are better citizens. With indirect funding, however, a drug treatment program with worship and Bible study at its core can receive government money.

There is a long line of court cases approving indirect funding for programs that include religious elements. These are the Supreme Court cases upholding vouchers to fund religious education. For example, in the *Zelman* case in the summer of 2002, the Supreme Court upheld the Cleveland voucher program that enables poor families to choose religious schools for their children.[17]

Vouchers and other forms of indirect funding are not very common in the area of social services. Most of the time the government awards grants or contracts to groups, and such direct funding comes with the rule that the government money cannot pay for any inherently religious activities. Officials can redesign government social service programs, however, so that the funding is indirect instead of direct. That change would allow faith-based programs that incorporate worship or Bible study to seek government support. It would also help out the needy by giving them an array of choices for service instead of being restricted to the one or two programs that receive a grant or contract.

Indirect funding will not become more widespread on its own though. Faith leaders will probably need to encourage government officials and elected representatives to become more creative in this area.

By the way, there is one area of policy where indirect funding is common—federally funded child care. Since 1990 states may use federal funds for child care to give certificates or vouchers to low-income families that enable the families to get care for their children at whichever day care provider they choose. Because the funding is indirect, there are no restrictions on the religious content of the day care—Congress was happy to accommodate the choice of parents who want little Johnny and Jane to hear about David and Goliath during story time. Faith-based day care providers are eligible to accept the certificates and then turn them in for payment if they meet a state's qualifications for day care providers.

So churches across the country are providing federally funded day care without religious restrictions. Parents are glad to have choices. States are glad not to have to administer thousands of contracts, and no anti-faith group has wasted time challenging the system as unconstitutional.

Collaborating without Government Funding

As famed O. J. Simpson attorney Johnny Cochran might say, "If it doesn't fit, you mustn't submit." If your ministry is a "brownie" ministry and the government funding is direct instead of indirect, or if some other condition of the government funds is too restrictive, or if your group just isn't ready to take on the burdens that come with government funding, then *don't do it!* No faith-based group is required to accept government money. Not at all. Rather the opposite: if the funding will undermine your mission, you should not take it. Search for other support, and trust that God will supply it.

Does that mean no collaboration with government? It shouldn't mean that. The mother your church is assisting may need the help of a government official to persuade the father who left to start supporting the kids, or she may need to become enrolled in the government program that gives out vouchers for child care. To know what kind of help the government offers, who is eligible for it, and where it is given, your staff needs to be acquainted with government programs. Building a relationship with social service officials enables you to better serve people who come to you for help.

Also, your program may offer just the kind of help that someone in a government-funded program needs. The local One-Stop Center might provide job training but not life-skills help, job placement services but not a job coach who can support the new employee in the new job. Such services, which are routinely offered by churches and parachurch groups, may be just what it takes for a person in the government's program to succeed.

One-Stop operators and welfare officials are often looking for nonfinancial partnerships with faith-based groups to which they can refer their clients for these additional services. Sometimes these referral relationships are very extensive—the Family Pathfinders program in Texas, for example, has involved hundreds of congregations.

What a wonderful contribution this is for faith-based groups to make to people the government is helping—and without the strings that come with government funds. So go talk to officials about what you do and how that can mesh with what they do. (Initiating that conversation is a good idea, too, to avoid the "one-way referrals" that sometimes occur when officials suggest that a needy family or person should visit your ministry but neglect to first talk with you about your capacity and capabilities.)

GOVERNMENT CAN'T SAVE YOUR SOUL

We have said it before and want to emphasize it strongly here again: although it is true that the government can tempt faith-based organizations to betray their religious mission by offering funding that comes with secularizing rules, the opposite is not true. The government cannot, by eliminating those secularizing rules, guarantee that a faith-based group will remain faithful. After all, faith-based organizations are quite able to lose their way without getting a cent of government money.

Of course, it is not the government's responsibility to keep your church or parachurch ministry faithful to its mission of serving the needy in a way that honors God. That is the responsibility of the faith-based organization itself—its staff, its board of directors, its volunteers, and its supporters.

Faithfulness requires something more than avoiding too much government money or working with a good lawyer to find and reject improper religious restrictions. It requires clarity of mission and clarity about how that mission should shape the program and staff. It requires persistence and care to ensure there is no drift from the mission as new people are hired, programs expand, or new methods are tried out. It requires a leadership that does not get bogged down in details and is not overly impressed by success stories and praise but constantly asks what the organization should be doing and how it can be doing it better. And faithfulness, of course, requires prayer.

JUST WHAT IS THE MISSION?

Thinking about government money, evangelicals spend a lot of time worrying about preserving the purity of the mission of their organizations. That is a vital concern—we just focused on it a few sentences ago. So it is worth thinking a bit about what purity of mission means when it comes to serving needy families and neighborhoods.

There is a temptation to judge purity of mission only internally—to just worry about having to modify a fine plan for service because officials say, for example, that prayer must be voluntary. That's an important measure of faithfulness, but not the only one. After all, the mission is to help neighbors and neighborhoods in need and not just to be true to an abstract plan or vision of service. It could be that the plans have to be modified in order to actually accomplish the mission of service. Might it be true that to faithfully serve our neighbors, we should change how and when we present the gospel or insist that staff be both expert and faith-filled? Being faithful to our mission of service could require rethinking our service ideas—not clinging to them because we think change must mean a loss of purity.

The greater opportunity that evangelical ministries have to receive federal funds to support their services can be seen as a temptation to go off course. It can also be seen as a challenge to prayerfully reflect again on how we can best serve our neighbors who need our help and our love.

Epilogue

he vast ballroom of the Marriott Hotel in downtown Philadelphia was packed with fifteen hundred people, representing a mosaic of faiths and ethnicities. Clergy and leaders of faith-based organizations waited in anticipation for President George W. Bush to arrive. Elected officials, dignitaries, and federal, state, and local civil servants were eager to hear what the president would say about an initiative that he has always said is close to his heart. It was 12 December 2002, in the middle of a conference for grassroots leaders, sponsored by the White House Office of Faith-Based and Community Initiatives.

The tension grew as photographers scrambled to set up cameras and microphones. Journalists stood by with tape recorders and notepads in hand. Then without warning, brass instruments struck up "Hail to the Chief" to the waiting crowd. Serious-looking dark-suited Secret Service agents formed a human fortress along the front. Moments later, the curtain opened and the president walked in waving to the exuberant crowd.

Indeed it was a magical moment. There was a sense that something significant was about to take place, but what would the president say? The movement to enlarge the role of faith-based help as part of the nation's compassionate outreach was popular with the public. Businesses and foundations were rethinking their traditional reluctance to work closely with religious programs. Academics and the press had discovered that much of the help needy people receive, and some of the most effective programs, are faith-based. United Way and local networks of nonprofits were seeing that grassroots groups, religious as well as secular, are important partners. Yet Congress had balked at extending Charitable Choice. Opponents of expanded faith-based services had tied up in the Senate a measure with strong bipartisan support to stimulate greater individual and corporate giving to charities and to end petty government restrictions against faith-based social service programs. Powerful groups claimed the president's effort to "rally the armies of compassion" was unconstitutional and designed to promote discrimination against nonreligious individuals and organizations. Even many of the president's Christian supporters had been skeptical.

Faced with this tide of opposition and opportunity, this is what the president said:

> We have work to do. We must be honest about it. We have got a lot of work to do in this country, because there are pockets of despair in America. There are men and women who doubt the American Dream is meant for them. There are people who face the struggles of illness and old age with no one to help them or pray with them. There are men and women who fight every minute of the day against terrible addictions. There are boys with no family but a gang, and teenage moms who are abandoned and alone. And then there are the children who wonder if anybody loves them.
>
> We've reformed welfare in America to help many, yet welfare policy will not solve the deepest problems of the spirit. Our economy is growing, yet there are some needs that prosperity can never fill. We arrest and convict dangerous criminals, yet building more prisons is no substitute for responsibility and order in our souls.
>
> No government policy can put hope in people's hearts or a sense of purpose in people's lives. That is done when someone, some good soul puts an arm around a neighbor and says, "God loves you, and I love [sic], and you can count on us both."
>
> And we find that powerful spirit of compassion in faith-based and community groups across our nation: People giving shelter to the homeless; providing safety for battered women; giving care and comfort to AIDS victims; bringing companionship to lonely seniors.
>
> . . . Faith-based charities work daily miracles because they have idealistic volunteers. They're guided by moral principles. They know the problems of their own communities, and above all, they recognize the dignity of every citizen and the possibilities of every life.

These groups and many good charities that are specifically religious have the heart to serve others. Yet many lack the resources they need to meet the needs around them.

They deserve the support of the rest of us. They deserve the support of foundations. They deserve the support of corporate America. They deserve the support of individual donors, of church congregations, of synagogues and mosques. And they deserve, when appropriate, the support of the federal government.

Faith-based groups will never replace government when it comes to helping those in need. Yet government must recognize the power and unique contribution of faith-based groups in every part of our country. And when the federal government gives contracts to private groups to provide social services, religious groups should have an equal chance to compete. When decisions are made on public funding, we should not focus on the religion you practice; we should focus on the results you deliver.

. . . In government, we're still fighting old attitudes, habits and rules that discriminate against religious groups for no good purpose. In Iowa, for example, the Victory Center Rescue Mission was told to return grant money to the government because the mission's board of directors was not secular enough. The St. Francis House Homeless Shelter in South Dakota was denied a grant because voluntary prayers were offered before meals. A few years ago in New York, the Metropolitan Council on Jewish Poverty was discouraged from even applying for federal funds because it had the word "Jewish" in its name.

These are examples of a larger pattern, a pattern of discrimination. And this discrimination shows a fundamental misunderstanding of the law. I recognize that government has no business endorsing a religious creed, or directly funding religious worship or religious teaching. That is not the business of the government. Yet government can and should support social services provided by religious people, as long as those services go to anyone in need, regardless of their faith. And when government gives that support, charities and faith-based programs should not be forced to change their character or compromise their mission.

And I don't intend to compromise either. I have worked for a faith-based initiative to rally and encourage the armies of compassion. I will continue to work with Congress on this agenda. But the needs of our country are urgent and, as President, I have an authority I intend to use. Many acts of discrimination against faith-based groups are committed by Executive Branch agencies. And, as the leader of the Executive Branch, I'm going to make some changes, effective today.

. . . Through all these actions, I hope that every faith-based group in America, the social entrepreneurs of America, understand that this government respects your work and we respect the motivation behind your work. We do not want you to become carbon copies of public programs. We want you to follow your heart. We want you to follow the word. We want you to do the works of kindness and mercy you are called upon to do.

For too long, for too long, some in government believed there was no room for faith in the public square. I guess they've forgotten the history of this great country. People of faith led the struggle against slavery. People of faith fought against child labor. People of faith worked for women's equality and civil rights. Every expansion of justice in American history received inspiration from men and women of moral conviction and religious belief. And in America today, people of faith are waging a determined campaign against need and suffering.

When government discriminates against religious groups, it is not the groups that suffer most. The loss comes to the hungry who don't get fed, to the addicts who don't get help, to the children who drift toward self-destruction. For the sake of so many brothers and sisters in need, we must and we will support the armies of compassion in America.[1]

When the president finished speaking, the applause was enthusiastic and long-lasting. Yet equally loud, and just as swift, were the cries in opposition from the critics of the president's faith and community agenda. Some groups vowed to use every legal means to stop the reforms. Others promised to continue opposition on Capitol Hill.

The Revolution of Compassion is a generation-long challenge and opportunity. It began before this administration and will continue on past it. It is occurring inside government and also in corporate boardrooms, in church basements and secular non-profit offices, in synagogues and mosques, in people's hearts. Yet after decades of pushing religious organizations to the margins, of ignoring the dynamic power of faith or considering it to be damaging, of excluding committed faith-based programs from funding or collaboration, it will take years to fully transform policies, laws, court decisions, and the attitudes of government officials, corporate donors, and foundation leaders.

On 12 December 2002, in Philadelphia, President Bush gave a powerful signal of his determination to continue this process of transformation. His words were not only a proclamation of how federal policies would change but a challenge to the nation as well, to the social sector, to business leaders, to citizens.

Ultimately, what is at stake is not federal funding. It is not just about delivering the most effective services; it is about discovering that we all have a calling to encourage and uplift our neighbors in need. America's way of reaching out has always included more than government action, and among its most important dimensions has always been the works of the faithful. Now, at the outset of a new century, we are all called to pioneer new partnerships and more effective acts of mercy and justice. We are all called to participate in a Revolution of Compassion.

Frequently Asked Questions

Q 1: *Why the focus on giving government money to faith-based groups when it is the church's responsibility, not government's, to help the needy?*

A: Many churches and parachurch ministries do assist poor and needy families. One goal of the faith-based initiative is to promote greater giving to such compassionate services. Government also assists the needy, however, mainly by giving money to private groups to support the services they offer. Views differ on how large government's role should be. In the meantime, the faith-based initiative insists that when the government does give funds to private service programs it must not discriminate against faith groups. They should have an equal chance to seek funding if they think the money will enhance rather than harm their programs.

Q 2: *Why doesn't the government just cut taxes so people can contribute more money to faith-based groups instead of trying to steer more government grants to those groups?*

A: A key strategy of leaders who favor a greater role for faith-based services is to change tax policy to encourage greater private giving. Yet government itself runs social programs to be sure even unpopular needs get help and that assistance will not disappear if private giving falters. The government mainly provides its social help by funding private service groups, and it should not discriminate against faith-based groups that provide effective assistance.

Q 3: *Why should people count on faith-based organizations, instead of the government, to supply social services?*

A: In fact, private service groups, including churches and parachurch ministries, have always been major parts of the American social safety net upon which the needy depend. Faith-based help has a unique power to transform lives, leading to permanent changes. So politicians, scholars, and policy analysts, even if they are not believers, are looking for ways to increase the role of faith-based services. Christians and other believers should be glad that public opinion and policy makers are acknowledging the important and positive role that faith plays in the lives of individuals, communities, and the social services. The faith-based initiative enlarges the importance of faith-based services without collapsing the government's role of overseeing and coordinating our society's response to need.

Q 4: *Isn't the idea of government partnerships with faith-based groups just a hidden way for the government to dump its social responsibilities on the doorsteps of the churches?*

A: There would be a problem of dumping if the government simply stopped its social spending and told needy people to find their way to some local church for help, but that's not what the faith-based initiative proposes. Instead, the initiative is ending the bias against faith that has been prevalent in many government programs that fund private social services. As discrimination ends, more faith-based social service programs are winning government money, but that's fair treatment, not government dumping of its social responsibilities on the churches.

Q 5: *If the federal government funds religious groups to provide social services, won't federal money end up going to groups whose beliefs we know are wrong?*

A: Think about the alternative: if the federal government only funds secular groups, then all that federal money will be going only to groups with the outlandish view that the body and mind are all that exist and faith is irrelevant when people are in need! That doesn't seem like a great solution. Because our Constitution upholds religious liberty and forbids an established religion—and because it wouldn't be right for government officials to pretend to be infallible theologians—the government will always be funding groups that one part or another of America considers religiously objectionable. Yet, if a group of a different faith does good work, such as helping a homeless family become self-supporting, shouldn't we be glad that the group successfully aided a needy neighbor? Remember, too, that the rules for government funding are designed to make it clear that the government—and our tax money—supports the good outcome and not the religious beliefs of the group. Government money can't be used to pay for tracts, for example. And also remember that officials will refuse to fund organizations that violate basic American standards of how people should be treated.

Christians concerned that programs based on objectionable beliefs will get funded should redouble their efforts to shape good programs so that officials have better choices. The practical issue is this: If excellent Christian ministries refuse to partner with the government, then officials will have no choice but to fund programs that reflect other faiths or that are ineffective and even harmful.

Q 6: *Doesn't the constitutional principle of the separation of church and state forbid the federal government from setting up a program just to give money to churches?*

A: There is no new program to give money to churches; there is no pot of money just for Christian ministries. Even though the U.S. Constitution does not actually include the phrase "separation of church and state," it does require government not to establish religion but to protect religious liberty. It would be wrong for the government to start paying to support churches, synagogues, and mosques. Government-supported religion has proven bad for both religion and government. It is equally wrong, however, for the government to support just secular programs when many good programs are faith-based. Officials should choose the best programs to receive government support; they owe it to taxpayers and the needy to have a bias for effectiveness. So the real issue is this: can officials give government grants to the most effective social services programs, whether religious or secular? If officials fund an effective church-related social program, they are using taxpayer money wisely, not turning the church into a taxpayer-supported institution.

Q 7: *Isn't the faith-based initiative just a cynical effort by the Republican Party to gain the votes of blacks and Hispanics?*

A: There may be some Republican strategists who favor the initiative for that reason, but President Bush was an early advocate of equal treatment when he was still governor of Texas. Besides, initiatives to expand partnerships with faith-based groups did not start with him. The faith-friendly Charitable Choice rules were put into the law four times under President Clinton, and during the 2000 presidential campaign both Democratic candidate Al Gore and Republican George W. Bush promoted Charitable Choice. In Congress and at the state and local level, some of the strongest advocates for faith-based reforms are Democrats—concern for equal treatment and effective social services is not a Republican monopoly. Politicians are finally acknowledging the reality that in many poor communities and communities of color, the main or only sources of hope and help are churches and church-based programs. The faith-based initiative is a policy idea that should be judged on its own terms—does it really create equal opportunity for all groups seeking funding, and are the poor in fact better served?

Q 8: *Isn't it foolish for faith-based groups to count on government funding, since the faith-based initiative will disappear when the federal administration changes hands?*

A: Faith-based groups should never build their entire strategy on getting government money but need diversified funding to preserve their independence. In any case, the faith-based initiative will not disappear when a new president is elected. Government has been addressing social problems for many decades almost entirely by funding private social service programs. The question simply is which private groups can take part. Although the courts used to say that government cannot "aid" religion, they now regard equal treatment of all groups, religious or secular, as the constitutional requirement. So government partnerships with faith-based organizations are not going to disappear. Efforts to expand those partnerships did not start with the Bush administration and are not even limited to the United States. Government officials, academics, and policy analysts who are concerned about effective social services regard policy changes that invite faith groups into partnership as a way to improve services for the needy. The faith-based initiative is a good-government reform and not the special interest of religious people.

Q 9: *How can the faith-based initiative advocate turning services over to religious groups when there is no proof these groups do a better job?*
A: There is no plan for the government to stop funding secular providers and start funding religious providers simply because the former are secular and the latter are religious. The plan is to remove artificial restrictions in the law that keep officials from being able to choose the most effective service providers, religious or secular. There is not much systematic research yet on the effectiveness of faith-based services, but neither is there much good research on the effectiveness of most secular service organizations. So more research is needed all around. In the meantime, there is no need to guess whether faith-based groups in general are better than secular providers. The practical question is always: which of the groups that have applied for government support will do the most good? No doubt some faith-based groups will rank at the top and others will not.

Q 10: *Why should the government take money away from experienced providers and turn it over to faith groups that do not have the experience or capability to manage funds carefully?*
A: No one is proposing to turn money over to faith-based groups just because they are faith-based or to ignore experience and capabilities. Yet no group should continue to get government money just because it always has gotten the money and has good relations with the funding programs. If ineffective groups lose their funding to newcomers who actually help the needy, we should all be pleased. Most of the faith-based groups that are now seeking government funding are not inexperienced—except at applying for government funding. They have been faithfully serving their neighbors for years on a shoestring. Rather than lower standards, the faith-based initiative includes wide-ranging efforts to expand the capabilities of faith-based (and secular) grassroots organizations—so they will be prepared to manage increased income. Sometimes, of course, the standards themselves are excessively complex and create unnecessary difficulties for all grantees. The faith-based initiative will cut rules that burden grantees without actually improving accountability or

results. That kind of change is good for all who apply for funding—and also for the people whom the funding is intended to help.

Q 11: *Won't denominations and religions start fighting each other when government officials favor one church or another in giving out government awards?*

A: Religious providers such as Catholic Charities, Lutheran Services of America, Jewish Federations, and the Salvation Army already get a lot of government money but without divisive conflict. Of course, if new groups apply for funds with the idea that they are owed a share, then there could be hostility. The faith-based initiative does not promise each faith group a piece of the pie. Officials will be looking for effective providers and not to reward a group merely because it is faith-based or belongs to a particular denomination. If the applicants focus on the best possible assistance for the people the money is supposed to help, then each should be pleased when the most effective programs win the funding, even if they are not the winners themselves. It is wrong for a group to interpret the outcome as government favoritism for one faith over another. For compassion to become more effective—the goal of the faith-based initiative—congregations and religious nonprofits have to focus on service and collaboration and not on enlarging their budgets with government money.

Q 12: *If the faith-based initiative is supposed to end discrimination against religious service programs, then why aren't groups that include worship or Bible study in their programs eligible for federal grants?*

A: Some effective programs help people overcome deep problems through religious transformation. According to the courts, the government cannot fund such programs with grants or contracts because it is not supposed to single out one religion or another for favors, but government can fund these programs indirectly. If the client, rather than a government official, chooses which group will provide the assistance and receive the government support, then it is clear that the government is not endorsing the group's faith, so the program can include discipleship training or worship. (Of course, the program still must really help clients with their problems and not just make them more religious.) Indirect funding is not yet used widely, but federally funded child care for poor families commonly uses the indirect funding mechanism of vouchers or certificates, so faith-based providers that meet state standards can participate without restrictions on their religious activities.

Q 13: *Won't faith-based groups inevitably use government money improperly for proselytizing?*

A: Mistakes are always likely in life. That is why the government monitors grantees, and groups have to have accountability policies. Of course sharing the gospel is not a mistake, although it is true that grant and contract money cannot be used for evangelism. In the United States, it is the responsibility of believers, not the government, to spread their faith. Faith-based groups that provide government-funded services have every right, though, to preach the Good News separately from the government-funded program and to invite participants from that program to voluntarily join in worship and study.

Q 14: *Should faith-based groups that take government money be able to hire whomever they wish, or is that merely government-funded job discrimination?*

A: When a faith-based group that is permitted by law to hire only believers is selected for a government grant, then the government is not funding job discrimination but simply making sure that taxpayer money goes to the most effective service organization. It is the faith-based organization, not the government, that is selecting employees on the basis of their faith commitment. When no government funding is involved, that is their right under federal civil rights law and under the laws of most states and local governments. Sometimes a condition of funding is that grantees must not use religion as an employment criterion, but that condition is not universal. Nor should it be. Faith-based groups that take faith into account in hiring and firing are only ensuring a staff compatible with their character and mission—just as environmental groups refuse to hire employees who do not care for God's good creation and Democratic senators don't pick Republicans to work for them. Even though the laws often, though not always, honor the liberty of faith-based groups to hire on a faith basis, actual discrimination is not permitted—selecting employees for irrelevant reasons such as a person's color, race, national origin, sex, or disability.

Q 15: *"With government shekels come government shackles," so won't faith-based groups that accept government money inevitably surrender to unacceptable government interference with their beliefs and operations?*

A: Faith-based groups do have to be on the alert not to accept excessively restrictive government rules. They have to be careful not to become so dependent on government money that they cannot walk away if some source of government funding comes with excessive restrictions. At the same time, they should culti-vate dependence on their true supporters—the folks in the pew and the neighborhood who will pray for them, volunteer their time and expertise, and donate out of their hard-earned income. Churches should probably establish a separate nonprofit orga-nization to accept the government funding and administer the services in order to protect the independence of the congregation itself. Some groups that pride themselves on informality and innovation might have to decide that the government's rules are just too limiting. But no one is simply inviting churches and parachurch ministries to subject themselves to improper restrictions. The faith-based initiative understands that, for faith-based groups to be welcome, the rules for government funding have to be made more welcoming.

Q 16: *If faith-based groups can retain their independence despite accepting govern-ment money, how will they be held accountable to follow the regulations, use the money properly, and actually make a difference?*

A: Retaining their autonomy simply means that the faith-based groups have the freedom to be faith-based, within constitutional limits, even as they enter into partnership with the government. If they enter into the partnership, however, they are responsible to perform up to the same standards as every other organization that accepts government funding. No one is required to take it on faith that a faith-based group is following the rules, properly spending the funds, or achieving results. If an audit is required of other grantees, or the curricula for training courses must be reported, or documentation of effectiveness offered, then the same is required of faith-based grantees. Under Charitable Choice, a church that provides services can keep auditors from roaming through the church's entire budget and operations by putting all the government money into a separate account, but that separate account is subject to the same auditing as the budgets of all other grantees. In any case, shouldn't Christian minis-tries be striving to be the most effective, transparent, and cost-effective? That would be a wonderful witness to the world.

Q 17: *Isn't the faith-based initiative really a hoax, because many new groups are being invited to get government funds but without an increase in the amount of government money?*

A: Whether or not the government budget for social spending increases, unjustifiable obstacles to participation by faith-based groups ought to be eliminated. No effective faith-based group should be excluded just because it is faith-based. Also, no inef-fective secular group should continue to get money just because it has traditionally been a favored partner of the government. When officials focus on the quality of services rather than on whether the provider is secular or "too religious," then the best providers will be chosen and ineffective providers will no longer be funded. Even if the amount of money does not change, the result should be better and more assistance for the same amount of government funding. We should all be glad if religious liberty is allowed to flourish because mistaken restrictions are elimi-nated. We also should be glad if the needy get more effective help because ineffective programs (faith-based or secular) are replaced by more effective programs (faith-based or secular). Then we can focus on another key question: Besides becoming more welcoming to faith-based and grassroots groups, should the government also spend more money on social services? It could be. As believers and other citizens get more engaged in reaching out to their neighbors, they'll be better able to see the desperate needs of some of those neighbors and more commit-ted to expanded help. And then we all will be better able to see how much private groups should do and what the government's own responsibilities are.

Faith-Based Ministries' Code of Conduct

he Code of Conduct is a way for faith-based groups to communicate to government, the public, clients, and faith communities how they will conduct themselves when they accept government funds. Providing effective services, giving value for money, treating all clients with respect, and being above reproach in all our dealings is what we require of ourselves, even without government contracts and requirements. You may wish to copy this code, sign it, and then use it as a basis for discussing financial cooperation with your government counterpart. Or you may want to use it to stimulate internal discussions about proper attitudes and procedures.

Code of Conduct

Compliance: We agree to abide by the regulations of Charitable Choice. We openly affirm that government legitimately asserts certain requirements and that, having agreed to accept the funds, we accept the duties attached (unless a gross injustice or issue of conscience would compel dissent). We commit to use only private funds, and never government contract funds, to underwrite inherently religious activities such as worship, sectarian instruction, and evangelism.

Truthfulness and Transparency: We commit ourselves to open, straightforward, clear, consistent communication about our religious identity to our volunteers, service beneficiaries, donors, and government. This means that our program descriptions will clearly depict our expectations of program participants, and explain which components of our programs are optional and which are mandatory. Our desire is to allow potential staff, volunteers, participants, and government contacts to make choices about involvement with our organization on the basis of full and accurate information about our program content, ethos, goals, and methodology.

Autonomy/Preservation of Religious Character: We celebrate our identity as a faith-based organization and affirm Charitable Choice's guarantee to protect our religious character. We agree to refrain from using government funds to underwrite instruction that seeks to convert people to our religious faith (e.g., confessional activities such as study of sacred texts or classes in religious doctrine), but we maintain our right to identify our faith perspective in our educational endeavors (e.g., inculcating morals consistent with the Bible).

Witness: We commit ourselves to a gentle and winsome public witness and to the creation of an environment in which staff, volunteers, and program participants are free to speak autobiographically about their own lives, including their faith. Our staff and volunteers are instructed to welcome and lovingly respond to spiritual inquiry and discussion initiated by program participants. The environment of our program and the behavior and demeanor of our staff and volunteers witnesses to our faith commitments. When a program participant wishes to explore inherently religious topics like salvation, Scripture interpretation, or worship, we will welcome the opportunity and arrange a time to do so outside the scheduled times of the government-funded program.

Love of Neighbor: We are committed to responding to our neighbors' diverse educational, vocational, financial, spiritual, emotional, and physical needs, treating each individual with dignity. We affirm "relational ministry" that helps poor and needy people to connect to personal support networks—e.g. mentoring relationships with church members or support groups affiliated with the person's religious tradition—equipped to offer them emotional and practical help. Participation in such groups, however, will never be communicated as a pre-requisite for receiving services. Our goal is to inform program participants of the options available to them for cultivating a personal network of support; they themselves must be free to determine whether or not to pursue those opportunities.

Freedom from Religious Coercion: We reject all forms of religious coercion and will not make the receipt of services contingent on the service beneficiary's participation in religious activities we sponsor. In programs underwritten with government funds, we pledge to refrain from making attendance in religious activities mandatory. We recognize that, for faith-based organizations operating rehabilitation programs in which participation in religious exercises is considered inherently vital to the participant's transformation (and in which participants freely agree to commit to the whole program), government contracts ought not to be sought, since these would require compartmentalizing program components. Rather, such programs should be funded fully by private means.

Nondiscrimination of Beneficiaries: We will offer our services to all persons in need, regardless of their religious affiliation (or lack of affiliation).

Mission Focus: We agree to pursue financial collaboration with government only for those ventures that clearly fit within our sense of mission and calling, rather than adding on program elements simply because there is government money available to fund them. We pledge not to silence our prophetic voice. Hence, we will not hesitate to criticize government just because we have a contract with government.

Evaluation: We commit ourselves to credible and objective evaluation procedures and to maintaining clear and documented participant records so as to facilitate proper assessment of program performance.

Golden Rule: We commit ourselves to avoiding turf wars, gossip, and negative posturing in our competition with fellow faith-based organizations in bidding for government contracts. Rather, we will treat our fellow religious and secular competitors as we ourselves want to be treated.

Financial Accountability: We affirm that, as recipients of public funding, we are accountable to God and to government. We will seek a standard of financial accountability and precision that is above reproach—including fully separate accounting of public and private dollars and transparency in financial practices.

Signature of Ministry Representative _____

Date _____

Reprinted with permission from Amy L. Sherman, *The Charitable Choice Handbook for Ministry Leaders* (Washington, D.C.: Center for Public Justice, 2001).

Recommended Resources

Ten Essential Websites

http://www.cpjustice.org
The Center for Public Justice is the best source of information on Charitable Choice and for insight on the faith-based initiative.

http://www.ccda.org
The Christian Community Development Association is the premier organization of church-related community-serving programs.

http://www.nationalservice.org
The Corporation for National and Community Service is a key federal government agency for mobilizing volunteers for social service.

http://www.hudsonfaithincommunities.org
The Faith in Communities Initiative of the Hudson Institute, headed by Amy L. Sherman, provides a wealth of information about how faith-based groups are ministering to their communities.

http://www.guidestar.org
GuideStar provides a current database of 850,000 nonprofit organizations that includes information regarding their operations, finances, etc.

http://www.performance-results.net
Performance Results, Inc., assists nonprofits with developing a plan
of action to measure the results of programs and services through
outcome-based evaluation (OBE).

http://www.religionandsocialpolicy.org
The Roundtable on Religion and Social Welfare Policy is an excellent source of news about faith-based issues and publishes guides
to research and to policy questions.

http://www.wecareamerica.org
We Care America is the first place to go for guidance about engag-
ing your church in social ministry, ministry models, and government
funding.

http://www.welfareinfo.org
The Welfare Information Network is the best source of news about
all aspects of welfare reform.

http://www.fbci.gov
The White House Office of Faith-Based and Community Initiatives provides much information on how the federal government is
changing to become faith-friendly. Its website also provides links to
the sites of the Centers for Faith-Based and Community Initiatives
in major federal social program-funding departments.

NONPROFIT FUNDING WEBSITES

Information on funding and grant writing for nonprofit organizations:

http://www.fdncenter.org
The Foundation Center

http://www.generousgiving.org
Generous Giving, Inc.

http://www.grantsmart.org
GrantSmart

CONNECTING FAITH-BASED PROGRAMS WITH CORPORATE AMERICA

Organizations that build collaborations between faith-based leaders and business professionals:

http://www.christianity.com/cma
Christian Management Association

http://www.stewardship.org
Christian Stewardship Association

http://www.fcci.org
Fellowship of Christian Companies International

http://www.halftime.org
Halftime, Inc.

LEGAL ASSISTANCE

The Center for Law and Religious Freedom of the Christian Legal Society (**http://www.clsnet.org**), 703–642–1070. Explain your concern and ask to be directed to a staff attorney or to one of the hundreds of CLS member attorneys throughout the country.

Gammon and Grange (**http://www.gandglaw.com**), 703–761–5000. Ask for Chip Grange, Mike Woodruff, Scott Ward, or Stephen Clarke. Will refer to local counsel if appropriate.

FURTHER READING

President George W. Bush's Faith and Community Agenda

Bush, President George W. "Rallying the Armies of Compassion." Booklet released by the White House on 29 January 2001. The booklet can be downloaded at http://www.whitehouse.gov/news/reports/faithbased.pdf (21 March 2003).

Loconte, Joseph. *God, Government and the Good Samaritan: The Promise and the Peril of the President's Faith-Based Agenda.* Washington, D.C.: Heritage Foundation, 2001.

Marvin Olasky. *Compassionate Conservatism: What It Is, What It Does, And How It Can Transform America* (New York: Free Press, 2000).

The White House. *Unlevel Playing Field: Barriers to Participation by Faith-Based and Community Organizations in Federal Social Service Programs.* August 2001. The report can be downloaded at http://www.whitehouse.gov/news/releases/2001/08/20010816-3-report.pdf (21 March 2003).

White House Office of Faith-Based and Community Initiatives. *Guidance to Faith-Based and Community Organizations on Partnering with the Federal Government.* December 2002.

Government Partnerships with Faith-Based and Community Groups

Cnaan, Ram A., with Robert J. Wineburg and Stephanie C. Boddie. *The Newer Deal: Social Work and Religion in Partnership.* New York: Columbia University Press, 1999.

Dionne, E. J., Jr., and Ming Hsu Chen, eds. *Sacred Places, Civic Purposes: Should Government Help Faith-Based Charity?* Washington, D.C.: Brookings Institution, 2001.

Glenn, Charles L. *The Ambiguous Embrace: Government and Faith-Based Schools and Social Agencies.* Princeton: Princeton University Press, 2000.

Johnson, Byron R. *Objective Hope: Assessing the Effectiveness of Faith-Based Organizations: A Review of the Literature.* Philadelphia: Center for Research on Religion and Urban Civil Society, 2002.

Lugo, Luis E. *Equal Partners: The Welfare Responsibility of Governments and Churches.* Washington, D.C.: Center for Public Justice, 1998.

Lupu, Ira C. and Robert W. Tuttle. *Government Partnerships with Faith-Based Service Providers: The State of the Law.* The Roundtable on Religion and Social Welfare Policy, December 2002.

Monsma, Stephen V. *When Sacred and Secular Mix: Religious Nonprofit Organizations and Public Money.* Lanham, Md.: Rowman & Littlefield, 1996.

Sider, Ronald J. "The Case for Discrimination." *First Things* (June/July 2002).

Streeter, Ryan. *Transforming Charity: Toward a Results-Oriented Social Sector.* Indianapolis: Hudson Institute, 2001.

Charitable Choice

Carlson-Thies, Stanley W. *Charitable Choice for Welfare and Community Services: An Implementation Guide for State, Local, and Federal Officials.* Washington, D.C.: Center for Public Justice, December 2000.

Davis, Derek and Barry Hankins, eds. *Welfare Reform and Faith-Based Organizations.* Waco: J. M. Dawson Institute of Church-State Studies, Baylor University, 1999.

A Guide to Charitable Choice: The Rules of Section 104 of the 1996 Federal Welfare Law Governing State Cooperation with Faith-based Social-Service Providers. Washington, D.C.: Center for Public Justice, and Annandale, Virginia: Center for Law and Religious Freedom of the Christian Legal Society, January 1997.

Hoover, Dennis R. "Charitable Choice and the New Religious Center." *Religion in the News* (Spring 2000).

Sherman, Amy L. *The Charitable Choice Handbook for Ministry Leaders.* Washington, D.C.: Center for Public Justice, 2001.

Churches Serving Their Communities

Carlson, Deanna. *The Welfare of My Neighbor: Living Out Christ's Love for the Poor, with a Workbook and Supplemental Guide by Amy L. Sherman.* Washington, D.C.: Family Research Council, 1999.

Sherman, Amy L. *Restorers of Hope: Reaching the Poor in Your Community with Church-based Ministries That Work.* Wheaton, Ill.: Crossway, 1997.

———. *The ABCs of Community Ministry: A Curriculum for Congregations.* Indianapolis: Hudson Institute, 2002.

Sider, Ronald J., Philip N. Olson, and Heidi Rolland Unruh. *Churches That Make a Difference: Reaching Your Community with Good News and Good Works.* Grand Rapids: Baker Books, 2002.

Skjegstad, Joy. *Starting a Nonprofit at Your Church.* Bethesda, Md.: Alban Institute, 2002.

More than Baby-Sitting: Ministering Through Child Care. One of a series of how-to manuals with videos. Crown Financial Ministries, http://www.crown.org.

Perkins, John M., ed. *Restoring At-Risk Communities: Doing It Together and Doing It Right.* Grand Rapids: Baker Books, 1995.

Queen, Edward L., II, ed. *Serving Those in Need: A Handbook for Managing Faith-Based Human Services Organizations.* San Francisco: Jossey-Bass, 2000.

Welfare Reform

Carlson-Thies, Stanley W. and James W. Skillen, eds. *Welfare in America: Christian Perspectives on a Policy in Crisis.* Grand Rapids: Eerdmans, 1996.

Gushee, David P., ed. *Toward a Just and Caring Society: Christian Responses to Poverty in America.* Grand Rapids: Baker Books, 1999.

Olasky, Marvin. *The Tragedy of American Compassion.* Washington, D.C.: Regnery Gateway, 1992.

Notes

CHAPTER 1: AMERICA NEEDS A REVOLUTION

1. Clayborne Carson, ed., *The Autobiography of Martin Luther King, Jr.* (New York: Warner Books), 220.

2. George W. Bush, *A Charge to Keep* (New York: Perennial-Harper Collins, 1999), 229.

3. Amy L. Sherman, "A Call for Church Welfare Reform," *Christianity Today,* 6 October 1997, 46–50.

4. Gerald Wisz, "Silence Is Golden: Urban Missions Fear What Government Money Could Buy," *World,* 9 March 1996, 17.

5. *Faith-Based Initiatives: Four Catholic Views* (Washington, D.C.: Faith & Reason Institute, 2001), 7.

6. Amy L. Sherman, "Who Are the Poor?" in *Sharing God's Heart for the Poor: Meditations for Worship, Prayer and Service* (Charlottesville, Va.: Trinity Presbyterian Church–Urban Ministries; Indianapolis: The Welfare Policy Center of the Hudson Institute, February 2000), 6.

CHAPTER 2: THE ROOTS OF REVOLUTION

1. Stanley Carlson-Thies, "Charitable Choice: Bringing Religion Back into American Welfare," in *Religion Returns to the Public Square: Faith and Policy in America,* ed. Hugh Heclo and Wilfred M. McClay (Washington, D.C.: Woodrow Wilson Center Press; Baltimore: Johns Hopkins University Press, 2003), 269–97.

2. Marvin Olasky, *The Tragedy of American Compassion* (Washington, D.C.: Regnery Gateway, 1992).

3. Alexis de Tocqueville, *Democracy in America,* trans. and ed. Harvey C. Mansfield and Delba Winthrop (Chicago: University of Chicago Press, 2000), vol. 2, part 2, chap. 5, 489.

4. Jonathan Edwards, quoted in Stephen Charles Mott, "Foundations of the Welfare Responsibility of the Government," in *Welfare in America: Christian Perspectives on a Policy in Crisis,* ed. Stanley Carlson-Thies and James Skillen (Grand Rapids: Eerdmans, 1996), 193–94.

5. Ram A. Cnaan, with Robert J. Wineburg and Stephanie C. Boddie, *The Newer Deal: Social Work and Religion in Partnership* (New York: Columbia University Press, 1999), 123–24.

6. Carlson-Thies, "Charitable Choice," 272.

7. Lester M. Salamon, *America's Nonprofit Sector: A Primer,* 2d ed. (New York: Foundation Center, 1999), chap. 8.

8. Stephen V. Monsma and J. Christopher Soper, eds., *Equal Treatment of Religion in a Pluralistic Society* (Grand Rapids: Eerdmans, 1998); Stephen V. Monsma, *When Sacred and Secular Mix: Religious Nonprofit Organizations and Public Money* (Lanham, Md.: Rowman & Littlefield, 1996).

9. Hugo Black, quoted in Stephen V. Monsma, "The Wrong Road Taken," in *Everson Revisited: Religion, Education, and Law at the Crossroads,* ed. Jo Renee Formicola and Hubert Morken (Lanham, Md.: Rowman & Littlefield, 1997), 124.

10. See especially Monsma, "The Wrong Road Taken."

11. Joe Loconte, *Seducing the Samaritan: How Government Contracts are Reshaping Social Services* (Boston: Pioneer Institute for Public Policy Research, 1997).

12. Michael W. McConnell, "Equal Treatment and Religious Discrimination," in *Equal Treatment of Religion,* ed. Monsma and Soper, 48.

13. Monsma, *When Sacred and Secular Mix.*

14. Mary Jo Bane and David T. Ellwood, *Welfare Realities: From Rhetoric to Reform* (Cambridge: Harvard University Press, 1994), 2–7.

15. Stanley W. Carlson-Thies, "Transforming American Welfare: An Evangelical Perspective on Welfare Reform," in *Toward a Just and Caring Society: Christian Responses to Poverty in America,* ed. David P. Gushee (Grand Rapids: Baker Books, 1999), 473–98.

16. Cnaan, *The Newer Deal.*

17. William Raspberry, "Then There Is Faith," *Washington Post,* 25 July 1997.

18. Joe Klein, "In God They Trust," *New Yorker,* 16 June 1997.

19. De Tocqueville, *Democracy in America,* vol. 2, part 2, chap. 5.

20. Lester M. Salamon and Helmut K. Anheier, *The Emerging Nonprofit Sector: An Overview* (Manchester, England: Manchester University Press, 1996), 1.

21. *Congressional Record,* 104th Cong., 1st sess., 1995, 141, pt. 142:S13500.

22. *1984 Equal Access Act,* 20 USC §4071; *Board of Education v. Mergens,* 496 U.S. 226 (1990); *Rosenberger v. Rector & Visitors of the Univ. of Va.,* 515 U.S. 819 (1995); *Bowen v. Kendrick,* 487 U.S. 589 (1988); *Agostini v. Felton,* 521 U.S. 203 (1997).

23. Carlson-Thies, "Charitable Choice"; Derek Davis and Barry Hankins, eds., *Welfare Reform and Faith-Based Organizations* (Waco: J. M. Dawson Institute of Church-State Studies, Baylor University, 1999); Dennis R. Hoover, "Charitable Choice and the New Religious Center," *Religion in the News* (Spring 2000).

24. This story is based on Jill Witmer Sinha, *Cookman United Methodist Church and Transitional Journey: A Case Study in Charitable Choice* (Washington, D.C.: Center for Public Justice, 2000).

25. *Personal Responsibility and Work Opportunity Reconciliation Act,* Public Law 104–93 (22 August 1996), Title I, §104 (42 USC §604a).

26. Amy L. Sherman, *The Growing Impact of Charitable Choice: A Catalogue of New Collaborations Between Government and Faith-Based Organizations in Nine States* (Washington, D.C.: Center for Public Justice, March 2000), 8–9.

CHAPTER 3: A NEW PARTNERSHIP

1. "Remarks as Prepared for Delivery by Vice President Al Gore on the Role of Faith-Based Organizations," 24 May 1999 (released by the Gore 2000 Campaign). Available as "Speech of Democratic Presidential Candidate Vice President Al Gore on Faith-Based Organizations, Delivered to the Salvation Army" at http://downloads.weblogger.com/gems/cpj/384.pdf (21 March 2003).

2. Information in this and the following three paragraphs is from President George W. Bush, "Rallying the Armies of Compassion," a booklet released by the White House on 29 January 2001. The booklet can be downloaded at http://www.whitehouse.gov/news/reports/faithbased.pdf (21 March 2003).

3. Mark Penn, "The Community Consensus," *Blueprint: Ideas for a New Century* (quarterly journal of the Democratic Leadership Council, Washington, D.C.), spring 1999, 53; Steve Farkas et al., *For Goodness' Sake: Why So Many Want Religion to Play a Greater Role in American Life: A Report from Public Agenda* (New York: Public Agenda, 2001).

4. George W. Bush, foreword to "Rallying the Armies of Compassion."

5. Joseph Knippenberg, "Democrats May Fear Loss of Party Faithful," *Atlanta Journal-Constitution,* 16 October 2002, 21A.

6. Jim Towey, quoted in Bill Sammon, "Bush Rolls Back 'Secular' Rules," *Washington Times,* 13 December 2002.

7. The White House, *Unlevel Playing Field: Barriers to Participation by Faith-Based and Community Organizations in Federal Social Service Programs* (August 2001). The report can be downloaded at http://www.whitehouse.gov/news/releases/2001/08/20010816-3-report.pdf (21 March 2003).

8. Executive Office of the President, Office of Management and Budget, *The President's Management Agenda* (released in 2001). The report can be downloaded at http://www.whitehouse.gov/omb/budget/fy2002/mgmt.pdf (21 March 2003).

9. Amy Sherman, *Collaborations Catalogue: A Report on Charitable Choice Implementation in 15 States* (Indianapolis: Hudson Faith in Communities, Hudson Institute, March 2002), 4. (The numbers aren't exactly accurate because it is impossible to get precise figures in every case.)

10. Kurt M. Senske, "Getting Rid of the 'Thou Shalt Nots'," *Fort Worth Star Telegram*, 4 February 2001; available on the Lutheran Social Services of the South website (http://www.lsss.org).

11. John C. Green and Amy Sherman, *Fruitful Collaborations: A Survey of Government-Funded Faith-Based Programs in 15 States* (Indianapolis: Hudson Faith in Communities, Hudson Institute, September 2002).

CHAPTER 4: IN PARTNERSHIP WITH BUSINESS

1. Authors' interview with Bob Buford, president of *Halftime* and Leadership Network, 19 November 2002.

2. Ibid.

3. Capital Research 2001 Report, *Patterns of Corporate Philanthropy: A Mandate for Reform.*

4. Ibid.

5. Wal-Mart website, http://www.walmart.com (November 2002).

6. Ibid.

7. Ibid.

8. Ibid.

9. Capital Research 2001 Report, *Patterns of Corporate Philanthropy.*

10. AT&T website, http://www.att.com (November 2002).

11. Ibid.

12. Bank of America website, http://www.bankofamerica.com (November 2002).

13. Authors' interview with Bob Buford, 19 November 2002.

14. Ram A. Cnaan, Center for Research on Religion and Urban Civil Society Report 2001 (Philadelphia: University of Pennsylvania, 2001).

15. Authors' interview with Tom McCallie, executive director, Maclellan Foundation, 19 November 2002.

16. Authors' interview with Bob Buford, 19 November 2002.

17. Ibid.

18. Ibid.

19. Maclellan Foundation website, http://www.maclellanfdn.org (November 2002).

20. Jim Collins, *Good to Great* (New York: Harper Collins, 2001), 10.

21. Authors' interview with Claudia Horn, president of Performance Results, Inc., 26 November 2002.

22. Collins, *Good to Great,* 85.

23. Authors' interview with Claudia Horn, 26 November 2002.

24. Michael Porter and Mark Kramer, quoted in Ryan Streeter, *Transforming Charity: Toward a Results-Oriented Social Sector* (Indianapolis: Hudson Institute, 2001), 130.

25. Ibid., 131.

26. Authors' interview with Claudia Horn, 26 November 2002.

27. Stephanie Strom, "Questions Arise on Accounting at United Way," *New York Times*, 19 November 2002.

28. Ibid.

29. Ibid.

30. Streeter, *Transforming Charity*, 32.

31. Leslie Kaufman, "New York Says Those on Welfare Are Increasingly Hard to Employ," *New York Times*, 29 November 2002.

32. Ibid.

33. *Working toward Independence: The President's Plan to Strengthen Welfare Reform*, February 2002, 16.

34. Jim Morill, Shariff Durhams, and Sarah Lunday, "Welfare That Works in Focus," *Charlotte Observer*, 27 February 2002, p. 1A.

35. Streeter, *Transforming Charity*, 33.

36. Amy Sherman, *Establishing a Church-based Welfare-to-Work Mentoring Ministry* (Indianapolis: Hudson Institute, 2000), 5.

37. Ibid., 17.

38. Jobs Partnership website, http://www.tjp.org, November 2002.

39. Bank of America Corporation press release, "Bank of America and National Jobs Partnership Form Strategic Alliance," 31 October 2001.

40. Ibid.

41. Ibid.

42. Gary Schneeberger, "From Welfare to Wellness," *Focus on the Family Citizen Magazine*, May 2001.

43. Suzanne Morse, quoted in Susan K. E. Saxon-Harrold and Aaron J. Heffron, "Crossing the Border: Competition and Collaboration Among Nonprofits, Business and Government," Independent Sector, theme issue of the *Facts & Findings* newsletter, vol . 1, no. 1 (2002), 2.

44. Saxon-Harrold and Heffron, "Crossing the Borders."

45. Bob Buford, "Bob Buford's Musings about His Own Activity in Philanthropy" (unpublished manuscript, November 1999).

46. Ibid.

47. Authors' interview with Mac McQuiston, president of CEO Forum, 21 November 2002.

48. "President Discusses Welfare Reform and Job Training," remarks by President George W. Bush to the Chamber of Commerce, Charlotte, North Carolina, White House Press Release, Office of the Press Secretary, 27 February 2002.

49. John J. DiIulio Jr., speech prepared for delivery and release before the National Association of Evangelicals, Dallas, Texas, 7 March 2001.

50. Authors' interview with Mac McQuiston, 21 November 2002.

51. Authors' interview with Bob Buford, 19 November 2002.

CHAPTER 5: COLLABORATING WITH THE SOCIAL SECTOR

1. William Booth, *In Darkest England and the Way Out* (Chicago: Charles H. Sergel and Company, 1890), 5–7.

2. *Salvation Army Year Book* (Salvation Army, Alexandria, Va., 1982), title page.

3. Charles Glenn, *The Ambiguous Embrace: Government and Faith-based Schools and Social Agencies* (Princeton, N. J.: Princeton University Press, 2000), 213.

4. Authors' interview wth Paul Bollwahn, October 2002.

5. Roger J. Green, *War on Two Fronts* (Atlanta: Salvation Army Supplies, 1989), 80.

6. Ibid., 84.

7. Philip Needham, "A Contemporary Theology of Social Service: Toward a Reintegration of The Salvation Mission," a paper presented at the Theology of Social Service Symposium, Winnipeg, Manitoba, 1984, p. 15.

8. Ibid., 3, 14.

9. Authors' interview with Paul Bollwahn, October 2002.

10. Glenn, *Ambiguous Embrace,* 219.

11. Paul Bollwahn, speech made during White House briefing, 30 May 2001.

12. Joe Loconte, quoted in Glenn, *Ambiguous Embrace,* 228.

13. Ibid.

14. Paul Bollwhan, "William Booth: The Development of His Social Concern" (booklet, Salvation Army, July 2000), 17.

15. Authors' interview with Paul Bollwahn, October 2002.

16. Ibid.

17. Diane Winston, *Soup, Soap and Salvation: The Impact of Charitable Choice on the Salvation Army* (Washington, D.C.: Center for Public Justice, May 2000), 9.

18. Glenn, *Ambiguous Embrace,* 223.

19. William Booth, quoted in ibid., 235.

20. Ibid., chapter 5; see also Cnaan, *The Newer Deal.*

21. Philip Needham, "The Domestic Partnership Issue: A Rational Response," *Salvation Army,* 2001.

22. Ibid.

23. Sharon Daly, quoted in Joe Loconte, *The Anxious Samaritan: Charitable Choice and the Mission of Catholic Charities* (Washington, D.C.: Center for Public Justice, May 2000), 11.

24. Loconte, *Anxious Samaritan,* 1.

25. Ibid.

26. Ibid., 1–2.

27. David Mills, correspondence with Dave Donaldson, 5 September 2002.

28. Marian L. Heard, Perspective column, *Leading the Way*, newsletter of the United Way of Massachusetts Bay, summer 1999, 3.

29. Glenn, *Ambiguous Embrace,* 239.

30. William Booth, quoted in ibid., 216.

Chapter 6: Equal Partners with Government

1. Cartoon by Mick Stevens, *New Yorker,* 16 April 2001.

2. Authors' interview with Bob Reccord, president of the Southern Baptist North American Mission Board, 26 November 2002.

3. Stephen Monsma, "Deciding Whether and When to Seek Government Funds," in *Serving Those in Need: A Handbook for Managing Faith-Based Human Services Organizations,* ed. Edward L. Queen II (San Francisco: Jossey-Bass, 2000), 175.

4. United Methodist Church, "Community-Based Ministries and Government Funding: A Response to Questions United Methodists Are Asking about Faith-based Initiatives" (General Board of Global Ministries, 2 June 2001), 45.

5. Amy Sherman, *The Charitable Choice Handbook for Ministry Leaders* (Washington, D.C.: Center for Public Justice, 2001), 16.

6. Monsma, "Deciding Whether and When," 178.

7. Ibid., 176.

8. See Clarke E. Cochran, "Accountability Guidelines for Government and Social Ministries" (Center for Public Justice, Washington, D.C., January 1998, photocopy).

9. Ibid., 10.

10. An excellent resource on why your church might want to set up a nonprofit and how it can do so is Joy Skjegstad, *Starting a Nonprofit at Your Church* (Bethesda, Md.: Alban Institute, 2002).

11. Monsma, "Deciding Whether and When," 178–79.

12. Ibid, 179.

13. Ibid., 176.

14. Amy Sherman, *Restorers of Hope: Reaching the Poor in Your Community with Church-based Ministries That Work* (Wheaton: Crossway, 1997), 217.

15. *Corporation of the Presiding Bishop v. Amos,* 483 U.S. 327 (1987).

16. Sherman, *Charitable Choice Handbook,* 13–14.

17. *Zelman v. Simmons-Harris,* 00-1751, decided June 27, 2002.

Epilogue

1. George W. Bush, "President Bush Implements Key Elements of His Faith-Based Initiative, Downtown Marriott Hotel, Philadelphia, Pennsylvania," 12 December 2002. The text of the speech can be accessed at http://www.whitehouse.gov/news/releases/2002/12/20021212-3.html (21 March 2003).

Dave Donaldson (M.A., Fuller Theological Seminary) is founder and CEO of We Care America, a national nonprofit organization that unites, strengthens, and multiplies effective social service ministries. The cofounder and former president of Convoy of Hope and past national director of Operation Blessing, Donaldson is chairperson of the Faith-Based Committee for Substance Abuse Treatment for the U.S. Department of Health and Human Services. An ordained minister, he served for three years as pastor of Adult Ministries for Canyon Hills Assembly of God, Bakersfield, California. He is a frequent guest on religious television and radio and speaks regularly for churches and leadership conferences around the world.

Stanley Carlson-Thies (Ph.D., University of Toronto) is the director of the Civitas Program in Faith and Public Affairs at the Center for Public Justice, Annapolis, Maryland. He also is a fellow of the Center for Public Justice and is former director of their Social Policy Studies group. Under the George W. Bush administration, he has served in various directorial roles for the White House Office of Faith-Based and Community Initiatives. His articles appear in numerous books and journals.

CAPITAL COMMENTARY

Regress, not Progress, in Georgia

Recent controversy over the President's Faith-based and Community Initiative has focused on one issue. When religious organizations receive government funds to provide services, do they have the right to hire only staff who share their deeply held religious beliefs? Should they be allowed to deny employment to people (say, homosexuals—or heterosexuals) who won't agree to respect an employer's faith-based behavioral standards? When the rights claims of individuals and faith-based organizations collide, how should the state intervene with justice?

This month the state of Georgia settled out of court the case of *Bellmore v. United Methodist Children's Homes*, a lawsuit brought by Lambda Legal Defense Fund, a gay rights group, that advanced the claims of a lesbian counselor and a Jewish therapist who sued a Christian organization for refusing to employ them. In a hasty settlement, the state agreed to require all faith-based childcare and child welfare programs that get state funding to forfeit their free-dom to use religious criteria in employment deci-

is simply non-negotiable. It's not uncommon. These organizations operate not unlike political campaigns that "discriminate" in hiring by choosing only true believers—committed Democrats or Republicans.

Second, this decision rolls back long-established civil rights of religious organizations to govern their hiring policies and internal affairs without government interference. Courts have repeatedly upheld the right of faith-based groups to use religion as a factor in hiring and firing decisions. No universal law or constitutional principle in the U.S. requires them to give up their freedom to hire staff fully committed to their religious mission when they use public funds. Sadly, not all states, cities, or federal programs honor this freedom. Civil rights progress requires more accommodation of religious staffing, not more restrictions.

Third, organizations in Georgia are now in a devilish bind. If a faith perspective leads them to build a

change their standards, any faith-based group with religious hiring policies will automatically be excluded from consideration for state contracts. Opponents of the faith-based initiative are now urging other states to follow Georgia's lead. They hail this as a "victory" for equality and individual rights.

But this is no victory. Instead, the state of Georgia is heading down a perilous path. The state's inability to defend an essential freedom of religious organizations will likely have several serious consequences. First, the state's decision to ride roughshod over legitimate religious freedom concerns will raise red flags for religious service groups, universities, and hospitals that have depended on this freedom for years. With this action, Georgia jeopardizes the possibility of forging respectful partnerships with organizations from many diverse faith traditions. For many groups, the right to hire staff members who share a common worldview or religious commitment

...they must either abandon that vision in order to join state programs or else abandon collaboration with the state in order to protect their religious mission. Georgia's new policy penalizes faith-based organizations for exercising what should be a positive, legally protected freedom. The playing field is not level if some organizations are disadvantaged simply for remaining true to their constitutionally protected convictions.

Georgia should have chosen a different path. The state should honor the right of all non-profit organizations (whether Christian or Jewish, pro-gay or pro-life, faith-based or secular) to hire the individuals they judge to be most qualified to fulfill their distinctive missions. This is not "discrimination." It is the only way to preserve the true diversity of America's social institutions, as well as individuals' rights to participate in a robust civil society.

—Stephen Lazarus
Senior Policy Associate

The Mission of the Center is to Equip Citizens, Develop Leaders, and Shape Policy in pursuit of its Purpose to Serve God, Advance Justice, and Transform Public Life.

The Center for Public Justice

P.O. Box 48368 * Washington, DC 20002 * 410-571-6300 * Fax 410-571-6365 * www.cpjustice.org * capcomm@cpjustice.org